A Gift for:

From:

for the MOMENT®

Inspiration for Each Day of the Year

Max Lucado

A Division of Thomas Nelson Publishers

Thomas Nelson
Since 1798

NASHVILLE DALLAS MEXICO CITY RIO DE JANEIRO

Published in Nashville, Tennessee, by Thomas Nelson. Thomas Nelson is a registered trademark of Thomas Nelson, Inc.

Thomas Nelson, Inc. titles may be purchased in bulk for educational, business, fundraising, or sales promotional use. For information, please e-mail SpecialMarkets@ThomasNelson.com.

Compiled and edited by Terri Gibbs

Editorial Supervision: Karen Hill, Executive Editor for Max Lucado

ISBN: 978-1-4003-2075-2

Printed in China

13 14 15 16 DSC 9 8 7 6

Contents

Preface

When I travel with my kids, I keep all the tickets in a satchel. When the time comes to board the plane or train, I stand between the attendant and the child. As each child passes, I place a ticket in her hand. She in turn gives the ticket to the attendant.

God does the same. He stands between us and our need, waiting to help us. For that reason the Bible says, "Let us boldly approach the throne of our gracious God, where we may receive mercy and his grace to find timely help" (Hebrews 4:16 NEB).

Did you note those last two words? "Timely help." Not too soon, nor too late. Just on time.

Just as it's my job to make sure my children have what they need, God will make sure you have what you need. From his hand you will receive "timely help."

And who knows, he may use these pages to give it.

Special thanks to Terri Gibbs for overseeing this project.

Also thanks to my friend and assistant Karen Hill for poring over the pages.

Appreciation goes to Jack Countryman for his enthusiastic support and great golf tips.

And to you, the reader. How kind of you to invite me into your world.

May God use these daily encounters to give you more of him—to give you grace for the moment.

Max Lucado
January 2000

Each Day . . .

It's quiet. It's early. My coffee is hot. The sky is still black. The world is still asleep. The day is coming.

In a few moments the day will arrive. It will roar down the track with the rising of the sun. The stillness of the dawn will be exchanged for the noise of the day. The calm of solitude will be replaced by the pounding pace of the human race. The refuge of the early morning will be invaded by decisions to be made and deadlines to be met.

For the next twelve hours I will be exposed to the day's demands. It is now that I must make a choice. Because of Calvary, I'm free to choose. And so I choose.

I choose love

No occasion justifies hatred;
no injustice warrants bitterness. I choose love.
Today I will love God and what God loves.

I choose joy

I will invite my God to be the God of circumstance.
I will refuse the temptation to be cynical . . .
the tool of the lazy thinker. I will refuse to see
people as anything less than human
beings, created by God.
I will refuse to see any problem as anything less than
an opportunity to see God.

I choose peace

I will live forgiven. I will forgive so that I may live.

I choose patience

I will overlook the inconveniences
of the world. Instead of
cursing the one who takes my place,
I'll invite him to do so.
Rather than complain that the wait is too long,
I will thank God for a moment to pray.
Instead of clenching my fist
at new assignments, I will face
them with joy and courage.

I choose kindness

I will be kind to the poor, for they are alone.
Kind to the rich, for they are afraid.
And kind to the unkind,
for such is how God has treated me.

I choose goodness

I will go without a dollar before
I take a dishonest one.
I will be overlooked before I will boast.
I will confess before I will accuse. I choose goodness.

I CHOOSE FAITHFULNESS

Today I will keep my promises.
My debtors will not regret their
trust. My associates will not
question my word. My wife will not question my love.
And my children will never fear that
their father will not come home.

I CHOOSE GENTLENESS

Nothing is won by force. I choose to be gentle.
If I raise my voice, may it be only in praise.
If I clench my fist, may it be only in prayer.
If I make a demand, may it be only of myself.

I choose self-control

I am a spiritual being. . . .
After this body is dead, my spirit will soar.
I refuse to let what will rot, rule the eternal.
I choose self-control. I will be drunk only by joy.
I will be impassioned only by my faith.
I will be influenced only by God.
I will be taught only by Christ.
I choose self-control.
Love, joy, peace, patience, kindness,
goodness, faithfulness, gentleness, and self-
control—to these I commit my day.
If I succeed, I will give thanks.
If I fail, I will seek his grace.
And then, when this day is done,
I will place my head on my pillow
and rest.

When God Whispers Your Name

JANUARY

I have chosen the way of truth; I have obeyed your laws.

—Psalm 119:30

January 1

God Listens

I cry out to the Lord; I pray to the Lord for mercy.

Psalm 142:1

You can talk to God because God listens. Your voice matters in heaven. He takes you very seriously. When you enter his presence, he turns to you to hear your voice. No need to fear that you will be ignored. Even if you stammer or stumble, even if what you have to say impresses no one, it impresses God, and he listens. He listens to the painful plea of the elderly in the rest home. He listens to the gruff confession of the death-row inmate. When the alcoholic begs for mercy, when the spouse seeks guidance, when the businessman steps off the street into the chapel, God listens.

Intently. Carefully.

The Great House of God

January 2

A Chosen People

You are a chosen people, royal priests, a holy nation, a people for God's own possession.

1 Peter 2:9

Do you ever feel unnoticed? New clothes and styles may help for a while. But if you want permanent change, learn to see yourself as God sees you: "He has covered me with clothes of salvation and wrapped me with a coat of goodness, like a bridegroom dressed for his wedding, like a bride dressed in jewels" (Isaiah 61:10).

Does your self-esteem ever sag? When it does, remember what you are worth. "You were bought, not with something that ruins like gold or silver, but with the precious blood of Christ, who was like a pure and perfect lamb" (1 Peter 1:18–19).

The challenge is to remember that. To meditate on it. To focus on it. To allow his love to change the way you look at you.

When Christ Comes

January 3

Worthless Worry

I was young, and now I am old, but I have never seen good people left helpless or their children begging for food.

Psalm 37:25

We worry. We worry about the IRS and the SAT and the FBI. . . . We worry that we won't have enough money, and when we have money, we worry that we won't manage it well. We worry that the world will end before the parking meter expires. We worry what the dog thinks if he sees us step out of the shower. We worry that someday we'll learn that fat-free yogurt is fattening.

Honestly, now. Did God save you so you would fret? Would he teach you to walk just to watch you fall? Would he be nailed to the cross for your sins and then disregard your prayers? Come on. Is Scripture teasing us when it reads, "He has put his angels in charge of you to watch over you wherever you go" (Psalm 91:11)?

I don't think so either.

In the Grip of Grace

January 4

A Complete Restoration

You will know that God's power is very great for us who believe.

Ephesians 1:19

God loves to decorate. God *has* to decorate. Let him live long enough in a heart, and that heart will begin to change. Portraits of hurt will be replaced by landscapes of grace. Walls of anger will be demolished and shaky foundations restored. God can no more leave a life unchanged than a mother can leave her child's tear untouched. This might explain some of the discomfort in your life. Remodeling of the heart is not always pleasant. We don't object when the Carpenter adds a few shelves, but he's been known to gut the entire west wing. He has such high aspirations for you. God envisions a complete restoration. He won't stop until he is finished. . . . He wants you to be just like Jesus.

Just Like Jesus

January 5

Don't Miss God's Answer

Is anything too hard for the Lord? No!

Genesis 18:14

The God of surprises strikes again. . . . God does that for the faithful. Just when the womb gets too old for babies, Sarah gets pregnant. Just when the failure is too great for grace, David is pardoned.

The lesson? Three words. Don't give up.

Is the road long? Don't stop.

Is the night black? Don't quit.

God is watching. For all you know right at this moment . . . the check may be in the mail.

The apology may be in the making.

The job contract may be on the desk.

Don't quit. For if you do, you may miss the answer to your prayers.

He Still Moves Stones

January 6

At Home with God

"If people love me, they will obey my teaching. My Father will love them, and we will come to them and make our home with them."

John 14:23

God wants to be your dwelling place. He has no interest in being a weekend getaway or a Sunday bungalow or a summer cottage. Don't consider using God as a vacation cabin or an eventual retirement home. He wants you under his roof now and always. He wants to be your mailing address, your point of reference; he wants to be your home.

For many this is a new thought. We think of God as a deity to discuss, not a place to dwell. We think of God as a mysterious miracle worker, not a house to live in. We think of God as a creator to call on, not a home to reside in. But our Father wants to be much more. He wants to be the one in whom "we live and move and have our being" (Acts 17:28 NIV).

The Great House of God

January 7

The Foundation of Courage

I will forgive their wickedness and will remember their sins no more.

Hebrews 8:12 NIV

Therefore, there is now no condemnation for those who are in Christ Jesus" (Romans 8:1 NIV).

"[God] justifies those who have faith in Jesus" (Romans 3:26 NIV).

For those in Christ, these promises are not only a source of joy. They are also the foundations of true courage. You are guaranteed that your sins will be filtered through, hidden in, and screened out by the sacrifice of Jesus. When God looks at you, he doesn't see you; he sees the One who surrounds you. That means failure is not a concern for you. Your victory is secure. How could you not be courageous?

The Applause of Heaven

January 8

The Water of the Servant

He poured water into a bowl and began to wash the followers' feet, drying them with the towel that was wrapped around him.

John 13:5

To place our feet in the basin of Jesus is to place the filthiest parts of our lives into his hands. In the ancient East, people's feet were caked with mud and dirt. The servant of the feast saw to it that the feet were cleaned. Jesus is assuming the role of the servant. He will wash the grimiest part of your life. . . .

If you let him. The water of the Servant comes only when we confess that we are dirty. Only when we confess that we are caked with filth, that we have walked forbidden trails and followed the wrong paths.

We will never be cleansed until we confess we are dirty. We will never be pure until we admit we are filthy. And we will never be able to wash the feet of those who have hurt us until we allow Jesus, the one we have hurt, to wash ours.

A Gentle Thunder

January 9

Our High Priest

Our high priest is able to understand our weaknesses. He was tempted in every way that we are, but he did not sin.

Hebrews 4:15

Read how J. B. Phillips translates Hebrews 4:15:

> For we have no superhuman High Priest to whom our weaknesses are unintelligible—he himself has shared fully in all our experience of temptation, except that he never sinned.

It's as if he knows that we will say to God: "God, it's easy for you up there. You don't know how hard it is from down here." So he boldly proclaims Jesus' ability to understand. Look at the wording again.

He himself. Not an angel. Not an ambassador. Not an emissary, but Jesus himself.

Shared fully. Not partially. Not nearly. Not to a large degree. Entirely! Jesus shared fully.

In all our experience. Every hurt. Each ache. All the stresses and all the strains. No exceptions. No substitutes. Why? So he could sympathize with our weaknesses.

In the Eye of the Storm

January 10

Made for Heaven

"My kingdom does not belong to this world."

John 18:36

Unhappiness on earth cultivates a hunger for heaven. By gracing us with a deep dissatisfaction, God holds our attention. The only tragedy, then, is to be satisfied prematurely. To settle for earth. To be content in a strange land.

We are not happy here because we are not at home here. We are not happy here because we are not supposed to be happy here. We are "like foreigners and strangers in this world" (1 Peter 2:11). . . .

And you will never be completely happy on earth simply because you were not made for earth. Oh, you will have your moments of joy. You will catch glimpses of light. You will know moments or even days of peace. But they simply do not compare with the happiness that lies ahead.

When God Whispers Your Name

January 11

Faithfully Present

"The Son of Man came to find lost people and save them."

Luke 19:10

Our God is the God who follows. Have you sensed him following you? He is the one who came to seek and save the lost. Have you sensed him seeking you?

Have you felt his presence through the kindness of a stranger? Through the majesty of a sunset or the mystery of romance? Through the question of a child or the commitment of a spouse? Through a word well spoken or a touch well timed, have you sensed him?

God gives us himself. Even when we choose our hovel over his house and our trash over his grace, still he follows. Never forcing us. Never leaving us. Patiently persistent. Faithfully present. He uses all his power to convince us that he is who he is and he can be trusted to lead us home.

The Gift for All People

January 12

Who Is the Servant?

Martha was distracted with much serving . . . "Mary has chosen that good part, which will not be taken away from her."

Luke 10:40–42 NKJV

Martha is worried about something good. She's having Jesus over for dinner. She's literally serving God. Her aim was to please Jesus. But she made a common, yet dangerous mistake. As she began to work for him, her work became more important than her Lord. What began as a way to serve Jesus, slowly and subtly became a way to serve herself. . . . She has forgotten that the meal is to honor Jesus, not Martha.

It's easy to forget who is the servant and who is to be served.

He Still Moves Stones

January 13

Thinking of You

Pray and ask God for everything you need, always giving thanks.

Philippians 4:6

Heaven knows no difference between Sunday morning and Wednesday afternoon. God longs to speak as clearly in the workplace as he does in the sanctuary. He longs to be worshiped when we sit at the dinner table and not just when we come to his communion table. You may go days without thinking of him, but there's never a moment when he's not thinking of you.

Knowing this, we understand Paul's rigorous goal: "We capture every thought and make it give up and obey Christ" (2 Corinthians 10:5). We can fathom why he urges us to "pray without ceasing" (1 Thessalonians 5:17 NKJV), "be constant in prayer" (Romans 12:12 ESV) . . . and "let heaven fill your thoughts" (Colossians 3:2 TLB).

The Great House of God

January 14

Just the Way You Are

In your lives you must think and act like Christ Jesus.

Philippians 2:5

It's dangerous to sum up grand truths in one statement, but I'm going to try. If a sentence or two could capture God's desire for each of us, it might read like this:

> God loves you just the way you are, but he refuses to leave you that way. He wants you to be just like Jesus.

God loves you just the way you are. If you think his love for you would be stronger if your faith were, you are wrong. If you think his love would be deeper if your thoughts were, wrong again. Don't confuse God's love with the love of people. The love of people often increases with performance and decreases with mistakes. Not so with God's love. He loves you right where you are.

Just Like Jesus

January 15

God's Good Gifts

Every good action and every perfect gift is from God.

James 1:17

Ever feel like you have nothing? Just look at the gifts [God] has given you:

He has sent his angels to care for you, his Holy Spirit to dwell in you, his church to encourage you, and his Word to guide you.
Anytime you speak, he listens; make a request and he responds.
He will never let you be tempted too much or stumble too far.
Let a tear appear on your cheek, and he is there to wipe it.
Let a love sonnet appear on your lips, and he is there to hear it.
As much as you want to see him, he wants to see you more.

You have been chosen by Christ. . . . He has claimed you as his beloved.

When Christ Comes

January 16

God's Good Timing

"God will always give what is right to his people who cry to him night and day, and he will not be slow to answer them."

Luke 18:7

Why does God wait until the money is gone? Why does he wait until the sickness has lingered? Why does he choose to wait until the other side of the grave to answer the prayers for healing?

I don't know. I only know his timing is always right. I can only say he will do what is best.

Though you hear nothing, he is speaking. Though you see nothing, he is acting. With God there are no accidents. Every incident is intended to bring us closer to him.

A Gentle Thunder

January 17

Clothes of Salvation

This body that dies must clothe itself with something that can never die.

1 Corinthians 15:53

Does Jesus care what clothes we wear?

Apparently so. In fact, the Bible tells us exactly the wardrobe God desires.

"But clothe yourselves with the Lord Jesus Christ and forget about satisfying your sinful self" (Romans 13:14).

"You were all baptized into Christ, and so you were all clothed with Christ. This means that you are all children of God through faith in Christ Jesus" (Galatians 3:26–27).

This clothing has nothing to do with dresses and jeans and suits. God's concern is with our spiritual garment. He offers a heavenly robe that only heaven can see and only heaven can give. Listen to the words of Isaiah: "The Lord makes me very happy; all that I am rejoices in my God. He has covered me with clothes of salvation and wrapped me with a coat of goodness" (Isaiah 61:10).

When Christ Comes

January 18
Sowing Seeds of Peace

Plant goodness, harvest the fruit of loyalty,
plow the new ground of knowledge.

Hosea 10:12

Want to see a miracle? Plant a word of love heart deep in a person's life. Nurture it with a smile and a prayer, and watch what happens.

An employee gets a compliment. A wife receives a bouquet of flowers. A cake is baked and carried next door. A widow is hugged. A gas-station attendant is honored. A preacher is praised.

Sowing seeds of peace is like sowing beans. You don't know why it works; you just know it does. Seeds are planted, and topsoils of hurt are shoved away.

Don't forget the principle. Never underestimate the power of a seed.

The Applause of Heaven

January 19

One Secure Place

"I will be with you always."

Matthew 28:20

David, the man after God's own heart, said: "I'm asking Yahweh for one thing, only one thing: to live with him in his house my whole life long" (Psalm 27:4 msg).

What is this house of God which David seeks? Is David describing a physical structure? Does he long for a building with four walls and a door through which he can enter but never exit? No. Our Lord "does not live in temples built by human hands" (Acts 17:24). When David says, "I will live in the house of the Lord forever" (Psalm 23:6), he's not saying he wants to get away from people. He's saying that he yearns to be in God's presence, wherever he is.

The Great House of God

January 20

A World Without Sin

Then wolves will live in peace with lambs, and leopards will lie down to rest with goats.

Isaiah 11:6

Can you imagine a world minus sin? Have you done anything recently because of sin?

At the very least, you've complained. You've worried. You've grumbled. You've hoarded when you should have shared. You've turned away when you should have helped.

Because of sin, you've snapped at the ones you love and argued with the ones you cherish. You have felt ashamed, guilty, bitter.

Sin has sired a thousand heartaches and broken a million promises. Your addiction can be traced back to sin. Your mistrust can be traced back to sin. Bigotry, robbery, adultery—all because of sin. But in heaven, all of this will end.

Can you imagine a world without sin? If so, you can imagine heaven.

When Christ Comes

January 21

A Heart Like His

We are like clay, and you are the potter; your hands made us all.

Isaiah 64:8

God wants us to be just like Jesus.

Isn't that good news? You aren't stuck with today's personality. You aren't condemned to "grumpydom." You are tweakable. Even if you've worried each day of your life, you needn't worry the rest of your life. So what if you were born a bigot? You don't have to die one.

Where did we get the idea we can't change? From whence come statements such as "It's just my nature to worry" or "I'll always be pessimistic. I'm just that way"? . . . Who says? Would we make similar statements about our bodies? "It's just my nature to have a broken leg. I can't do anything about it." Of course not. If our bodies malfunction, we seek help. Shouldn't we do the same with our hearts? Shouldn't we seek aid for our sour attitudes? Can't we request treatment for our selfish tirades? Of course we can. Jesus can change our hearts. He wants us to have a heart like his.

Just Like Jesus

January 22

The Reachable Jesus

He remembered us when we were in trouble. His love continues forever.

Psalm 136:23

God chose to reveal himself through a human body.

The tongue that called forth the dead was a human one. The hand that touched the leper had dirt under its nails. The feet upon which the woman wept were calloused and dusty. And his tears—oh, don't miss the tears—they came from a heart as broken as yours or mine ever has been.

So, people came to him. My, how they came to him! They came at night; they touched him as he walked down the street; they followed him around the sea; they invited him into their homes and placed their children at his feet. Why? Because he refused to be a statue in a cathedral or a priest in an elevated pulpit. He chose instead to be a touchable, approachable, reachable Jesus.

God Came Near

January 23

Blessings at God's Table

You prepare a meal for me in front of my enemies.

Psalm 23:5

Pause and envision the scene in [God's] royal dining room.

Driven not by our beauty but by his promise, he calls us to himself and invites us to take a permanent place at his table. . . . We take our place next to the other sinners-made-saints, and we share in God's glory.

> May I share a partial list of what awaits you at his table?
> You are beyond condemnation (Romans 8:1 NKJV).
> You are a member of his kingdom (Colossians 1:13).
> You have been adopted (Romans 8:15 NKJV).
> You have access to God at any moment (Ephesians 2:18 NKJV).
> You will never be abandoned (Hebrews 13:5).
> You have an imperishable inheritance (1 Peter 1:4).

In the Grip of Grace

January 24
The Compassionate Christ

When he arrived, he saw a great crowd waiting. He felt sorry for them. . . . So he began to teach them many things.

Mark 6:34

When Jesus lands on the shore of Bethsaida, he leaves the Sea of Galilee and steps into a sea of humanity. Keep in mind, he has crossed the sea to get away from the crowds. He needs to grieve. He longs to relax with his followers. He needs anything but another crowd of thousands to teach and heal.

But his love for people overcomes his need for rest.

Many of those he healed would never say "thank you," but he healed them anyway. Most would be more concerned with being healthy than being holy, but he healed them anyway. Some of those who asked for bread today would cry for his blood a few months later, but he healed them anyway. He had compassion for them.

In the Eye of the Storm

January 25

Adopted by God

The Spirit Himself bears witness with our spirit that we are children of God.

Romans 8:16 NASB

When we come to Christ, God not only forgives us, he also adopts us. Through a dramatic series of events, we go from condemned orphans with no hope to adopted children with no fear. Here is how it happens. You come before the judgment seat of God full of rebellion and mistakes. Because of his justice he cannot dismiss your sin, but because of his love he cannot dismiss you. So, in an act which stunned the heavens, he punished himself on the cross for your sins. God's justice and love are equally honored. And you, God's creation, are forgiven. But the story doesn't end with God's forgiveness.

It would be enough if God just cleansed your name, but he does more. He gives you his name.

The Great House of God

January 26

Guard Your Attitude

May our Lord Jesus Christ himself and God our Father encourage you and strengthen you in every good thing you do and say.

2 Thessalonians 2:16

Lord, don't you care that my sister has left me alone to do all the work?" (Luke 10:40).

Martha's life was cluttered. She needed a break. "Martha, Martha, you are worried and upset about many things," the Master explained to her. "Only one thing is important. Mary has chosen [it]" (Luke 10:41–42).

What had Mary chosen? She had chosen to sit at the feet of Christ. God is more pleased with the quiet attention of a sincere servant than the noisy service of a sour one.

What matters more than the type of service is the heart behind the service. A bad attitude spoils the gift we leave on the altar for God.

He Still Moves Stones

January 27

You're Something Special

Nothing . . . in the whole world will ever be able to separate us from the love of God.

Romans 8:39

We want to know how long God's love will endure. . . . Not just on Easter Sunday when our shoes are shined and our hair is fixed. Not when I'm peppy and positive and ready to tackle world hunger. Not then. I know how he feels about me then. Even I like me then.

I want to know how he feels about me when I snap at anything that moves, when my thoughts are gutter level, when my tongue is sharp enough to slice a rock. How does he feel about me then?

Can anything separate us from the love Christ has for us?

God answered our question before we asked it. So we'd see his answer, he lit the sky with a star. So we'd hear it, he filled the night with a choir; and so we'd believe it, he did what no man had ever dreamed. He became flesh and dwelt among us.

He placed his hand on the shoulder of humanity and said, "You're something special."

In the Grip of Grace

January 28

A Hunch and a Hope

"Daughter, your faith has made you well. Go in peace, and be healed of your affliction.'

Mark 5:34 NKJV

Maybe all you have [is] a crazy hunch and a high hope. You have nothing to give. But you are hurting. And all you have to offer him is your hurt.

Maybe that has kept you from coming to God. Oh, you've taken a step or two in his direction. But then you saw the other people around him. They seemed so clean, so neat, so trim and fit in their faith. And when you saw them, they blocked your view of him. So you stepped back.

If that describes you, note carefully . . . one person [whom Christ] commended . . . for having faith. It wasn't a wealthy giver. It wasn't a loyal follower. It wasn't an acclaimed teacher. It was a shame-struck, penniless outcast—[a woman who had been bleeding for twelve years]—who clutched onto her hunch that he could and her hope that he would.

Which, by the way, isn't a bad definition of faith. A conviction that he can and a hope that he will.

He Still Moves Stones

January 29

A Heart at Peace

The wisdom that comes from God is first of all pure, then peaceful, gentle, and easy to please.

James 3:17

The heart of Jesus was pure. The Savior was adored by thousands, yet content to live a simple life. He was cared for by women (Luke 8:1–3), yet never accused of lustful thoughts; scorned by his own creation, but willing to forgive them before they even requested his mercy. Peter, who traveled with Jesus for three and a half years, described him as a "lamb unblemished and spotless" (1 Peter 1:19 NASB).

After spending the same amount of time with Jesus, John concluded, "And in him is no sin" (1 John 3:5 NIV).

Jesus' heart was peaceful. The disciples fretted over the need to feed the thousands, but not Jesus. He thanked God for the problem. The disciples shouted for fear in the storm, but not Jesus. He slept through it. Peter drew his sword to fight the soldiers, but not Jesus. He lifted his hand to heal. His heart was at peace.

Just Like Jesus

January 30

God Heals Our Hurts

He had compassion on them.

Matthew 14:14 niv

The Greek word for compassion is *splanchnizomai*, which won't mean much to you unless you are in the health professions and studied "splanchnology" in school. If so, you remember that "splanchnology" is a study of the gut.

When Matthew writes that Jesus had compassion on the people, he is not saying that Jesus felt casual pity for them. No, the term is far more graphic. Matthew is saying that Jesus felt their hurt in his gut:

He felt the limp of the crippled.
He felt the hurt of the diseased.
He felt the loneliness of the leper.
He felt the embarrassment of the sinful.
And once he felt their hurts, he couldn't help but heal their hurts.

In the Eye of the Storm

January 31

The Lord Is Peace

God's peace, which is so great we cannot understand it, will keep your hearts and minds in Christ Jesus.

Philippians 4:7

The Lord came to Gideon and told him he was to lead his people in victory over the Midianites. That's like God telling a housewife to stand up to her abusive husband or a high school student to take on drug peddlers or a preacher to preach the truth to a congregation of Pharisees. "Y-y-you b-b-better get somebody else," we stammer. But then God reminds us that he knows we can't, but he can, and to prove it he gives a wonderful gift. He brings a spirit of peace. A peace before the storm. A peace beyond logic. He gave it to David after he showed him Goliath; he gave it to Saul after he showed him the gospel; he gave it to Jesus after he showed him the cross. And he gave it to Gideon. So Gideon, in turn, gave the name to God. He built an altar and named it *Jehovah-shalom*, "the Lord is peace" (Judges 6:24).

The Great House of God

FEBRUARY

The Lord is close to everyone who prays to him, to all who truly pray to him.

—Psalm 145:18

February 1

The Greenhouse of the Heart

People harvest only what they plant.

Galatians 6:7

Think for a moment of your heart as a greenhouse. And your heart, like a greenhouse, has to be managed.

Consider for a moment your thoughts as seeds. Some thoughts become flowers. Others become weeds. Sow seeds of hope and enjoy optimism. Sow seeds of doubt and expect insecurity.

The proof is everywhere you look. Ever wonder why some people have the Teflon capacity to resist negativism and remain patient, optimistic, and forgiving? Could it be that they have diligently sown seeds of goodness and are enjoying the harvest?

Ever wonder why others have such a sour outlook? Such a gloomy attitude? You would, too, if your heart were a greenhouse of weeds and thorns.

Just Like Jesus

February 2

Holiness Among Us

"Shout and be glad, Jerusalem. I am coming, and I will live among you," says the Lord.

Zechariah 2:10

God became a baby. He entered a world . . . of problems and heartaches.

"The Word became human and made his home among us. He was full of unfailing love and faithfulness" (John 1:14 NLT).

The operative word of the verse is *among.* He lived among us. He donned the costliest of robes: a human body. He made a throne out of a manger and a royal court out of some cows. He took a common name—*Jesus*—and made it holy. He took common people and made them the same. He could have lived over us or away from us. But he didn't. He lived among us.

He became a friend of the sinner and brother of the poor.

When Christ Comes

February 3

YOUR DAY IS COMING

"Hold on to what you have, so that no one will take your crown."

REVELATION 3:11 NIV

SOME OF YOU HAVE NEVER WON A PRIZE IN YOUR LIFE. Oh, maybe you were quartermaster in your Boy Scout troop or in charge of sodas at the homeroom Christmas party, but that's about it. You've never won much. You've watched the Mark McGwires of this world carry home the trophies and walk away with the ribbons. All you have are "almosts" and "what ifs."

If that hits home, then you'll cherish this promise: "And when the Chief Shepherd appears, you will receive the crown of glory that will never fade away" (1 Peter 5:4 NIV).

Your day is coming. What the world has overlooked, your Father has remembered, and sooner than you can imagine, you will be blessed by him.

WHEN CHRIST COMES

February 4
God's Help Is Near

The Lord *is close to everyone who prays to him, to all who truly pray to him.*

Psalm 145:18

Healing begins when we do something. Healing begins when we reach out. Healing starts when we take a step.

God's help is near and always available, but it is only given to those who seek it. Nothing results from apathy.

God honors radical, risk-taking faith.

When arks are built, lives are saved. When soldiers march, Jerichos tumble. When staffs are raised, seas still open. When a lunch is shared, thousands are fed. And when a garment is touched—whether by the hand of an anemic woman in Galilee or by the prayers of a beggar in Bangladesh—Jesus stops. He stops and responds.

He Still Moves Stones

February 5

God of Purpose

"He came to serve others and to give his life as a ransom for many people."

Matthew 20:28

Jesus refused to be guided by anything other than his high call. His heart was purposeful. Most lives aim at nothing in particular and achieve it. Jesus aimed at one goal—to save humanity from its sin. He could summarize his life with one sentence: "The Son of Man came to seek and to save the lost" (Luke 19:10 rsv). Jesus was so focused on his task that he knew when to say, "It is finished" (John 19:30). But he was not so focused on his goal that he was unpleasant.

Quite the contrary. How pleasant were his thoughts! Children couldn't resist Jesus. He could find beauty in lilies, joy in worship, and possibilities in problems. He would spend days with multitudes of sick people and still feel sorry for them. He spent over three decades wading through the muck and mire of our sin yet still saw enough beauty in us to die for our mistakes.

Just Like Jesus

February 6

God Always Gives Grace

For God all things are possible.

Mark 10:27

Our questions betray our lack of understanding:

How can God be everywhere at one time? (Who says God is bound by a body?)

How can God hear all the prayers which come to him? (Perhaps his ears are different from yours.)

How can God be the Father, the Son, and the Holy Spirit? (Could it be that heaven has a different set of physics than earth?)

If people down here won't forgive me, how much more am I guilty before a holy God? (Oh, just the opposite. God is always able to give grace when we humans can't—he invented it.)

The Great House of God

February 7

A Home for Your Heart

Lord, I love the Temple where you live, where your glory is.

Psalm 26:8

When it comes to resting your soul, there is no place like the Great House of God. "I'm asking Yahweh for one thing," [David] wrote, "only one thing: to live with him in his house my whole life long. I'll contemplate his beauty; I'll study at his feet. That's the only quiet, secure place in a noisy world" (Psalm 27:4–5 msg).

If you could ask God for one thing, what would you request? David said what he would ask. He longed to *live* in the house of God. I emphasize the word *live* because it deserves to be emphasized. David didn't want to chat. He didn't desire a cup of coffee on the back porch. He didn't ask for a meal or to spend an evening in God's house. He wanted to move in with him . . . forever. He was asking for his own room . . . permanently. He didn't want to be stationed in God's house; he longed to retire there. He didn't seek a temporary assignment but rather lifelong residence.

The Great House of God

February 8

Jesus Understands

He took our suffering on him and felt our pain for us.

Isaiah 53:4

Jesus knows how you feel. You're under the gun at work? Jesus knows how you feel. You've got more to do than is humanly possible? So did he. People take more from you than they give? Jesus understands. Your teenagers won't listen? Your students won't try? Jesus knows how you feel.

You are precious to him. So precious that he became like you so that you would come to him.

When you struggle, he listens. When you yearn, he responds. When you question, he hears. He has been there.

In the Eye of the Storm

February 9

A Letter of Joy

Rejoice in the Lord always. Again I will say, rejoice!

PHILIPPIANS 4:4 NKJV

GO WITH ME BACK IN HISTORY A COUPLE OF THOUSAND years. Let's go to Rome to a rather drab little room, surrounded by high walls. Inside we see a man seated on the floor. He's an older fellow, shoulders stooped and balding. Chains are on his hands and feet.

It is the apostle Paul; the apostle who was bound only by the will of God is now in chains—stuck in a dingy house—attached to a Roman officer.

He is writing a letter. No doubt it is a complaint letter to God. No doubt it is a list of grievances. He has every reason to be bitter and complain. But he doesn't. Instead, he writes a letter that two thousand years later is still known as the treatise on joy—Philippians.

Why don't you spend some time with it?

THE INSPIRATIONAL STUDY BIBLE

February 10

Preparing the Heart

As far as the east is from the west, so far has
He removed our transgressions from us.

Psalm 103:12 NKJV

Confession does for the soul what preparing the land does for the field. Before the farmer sows the seed, he works the acreage, removing the rocks and pulling the stumps. He knows that seed grows better if the land is prepared. Confession is the act of inviting God to walk the acreage of our hearts.

"There is a rock of greed over here. Father, I can't budge it. And that tree of guilt near the fence? Its roots are long and deep. And may I show you some dry soil, too crusty for seed?" God's seed grows better if the soil of the heart is cleared.

And so the Father and the Son walk the field together; digging and pulling, preparing the heart for fruit. Confession invites the Father to work the soil of the soul.

In the Grip of Grace

February 11

A Morsel of Kindness

Suppose someone has enough to live and sees a brother or sister in need, but does not help. Then God's love is not living in that person.

1 John 3:17

Leo Tolstoy, the great Russian writer, tells of the time he was walking down the street and passed a beggar. Tolstoy reached into his pocket to give the beggar some money, but his pocket was empty. Tolstoy turned to the man and said, "I'm sorry, my brother, but I have nothing to give."

The beggar brightened and said, "You have given me more than I asked for—you have called me brother."

To the loved, a word of affection is a morsel, but to the love-starved, a word of affection can be a feast.

He Still Moves Stones

February 12

See What God Has Done!

The heavens declare the glory of God.

Psalm 19:1

How vital that we pray, armed with the knowledge that God is in heaven. Pray with any lesser conviction and your prayers are timid, shallow, and hollow. But spend some time walking in the workshop of the heavens, seeing what God has done, and watch how your prayers are energized.

Behold the sun! Every square yard of the sun is constantly emitting 130,000 horsepower, or the equivalent of 450 eight-cylinder automobile engines. And yet our sun, as powerful as it is, is but one minor star in the 100 billion orbs which make up our Milky Way galaxy. Hold a dime in your fingers and extend it arm's length toward the sky, allowing it to eclipse your vision, and you will block out fifteen million stars from your view. By showing us the heavens, Jesus is showing us his Father's workshop. He taps us on the shoulder and says, "Your Father can handle that for you."

The Great House of God

February 13

The Voice of Adventure

"Those who try to keep their lives will lose them. But those who give up their lives will save them."

Luke 17:33

There is a rawness and a wonder to life. Pursue it. Hunt for it. Sell out to get it. Don't listen to the whines of those who have settled for a second-rate life and want you to do the same so they won't feel guilty. Your goal is not to live long; it's to live.

Jesus says the options are clear. On one side there is the voice of safety. You can build a fire in the hearth, stay inside, and stay warm and dry and safe.

Or you can hear the voice of adventure—God's adventure. Instead of building a fire in your hearth, build a fire in your heart. Follow God's impulses. Adopt the child. Move overseas. Teach the class. Change careers. Run for office. Make a difference. Sure it isn't safe, but what is?

He Still Moves Stones

February 14

Your Personal Blessing

God will praise each one of them.

1 Corinthians 4:5

What an incredible sentence. *God will praise each one of them.* Not "the best of them" nor "a few of them" nor "the achievers among them," but "God will praise each one of them."

You won't be left out. God will see to that. In fact, God himself will give the praise. When it comes to giving recognition, God does not delegate the job. Michael doesn't hand out the crowns. Gabriel doesn't speak on behalf of the throne. God himself does the honors. God himself will praise his children.

And what's more, the praise is personal! . . . Awards aren't given a nation at a time, a church at a time, or a generation at a time. The crowns are given one at a time. God himself will look you in the eye and bless you with the words, "Well done, good and faithful servant!" (Matthew 25:23 NIV).

When Christ Comes

February 15

The Heart of Jesus

"The Son does whatever the Father does."

John 5:19

The crowning attribute of Christ was this: his heart was spiritual. His thoughts reflected his intimate relationship with the Father. "I am in the Father and the Father is in me," he stated (John 14:11).

Jesus took his instructions from God. It was his habit to go to worship (Luke 4:16). It was his practice to memorize Scripture (Luke 4:4). Luke says Jesus "often slipped away to be alone so he could pray" (Luke 5:16). His times of prayer guided him. He once returned from prayer and announced it was time to move to another city (Mark 1:38). Another time of prayer resulted in the selection of the disciples (Luke 6:12–13). Jesus was led by an unseen hand.

The heart of Jesus was spiritual.

Just Like Jesus

February 16

SACRED DELIGHT

"Those people who know they have great spiritual needs are happy, because the kingdom of heaven belongs to them."

MATTHEW 5:3

GOD PROMISES SACRED DELIGHT. AND HE PROMISES IT to an unlikely crowd:

- "The poor in spirit." Beggars in God's soup kitchen
- "Those who mourn." Sinners Anonymous bound together by the truth of their introduction: "Hi, I am me. I'm a sinner."
- "The merciful." Winners of the million-dollar lottery who share the prize with their enemies
- "The pure in heart." Physicians who love lepers and escape infection
- "The peacemakers." Architects who build bridges with wood from a Roman cross . . .
- "The persecuted." Those who manage to keep an eye on heaven while walking through hell on earth

It is to this band of pilgrims that God promises a special blessing. A heavenly joy. A sacred delight.

THE APPLAUSE OF HEAVEN

February 17

The Sum of Christianity

"I did this as an example so that you should do as I have done for you."

John 13:15

Mark it down. We are what we see. If we see only ourselves, our tombstones will have the same epitaph Paul used to describe enemies of Christ: "Their god is their own appetite, they glory in their shame, and this world is the limit of their horizon" (Philippians 3:19).

Humans were never meant to dwell in the stale fog of the lowlands with no vision of their Creator.

Seeing Jesus is what Christianity is all about. Christian service, in its purest form, is nothing more than imitating him whom we see. To see his majesty and to imitate him, that is the sum of Christianity.

God Came Near

February 18

God Cares About You

"Look at the birds in the air. They don't plant or harvest or store food in barns, but your heavenly Father feeds them."

Matthew 6:26

Consider the earth! Our globe's weight has been estimated at six sextillion tons (a six with twenty-one zeroes). Yet it is precisely tilted at twenty-three degrees; any more or any less and our seasons would be lost in a melted polar flood. Though our globe revolves at the rate of one-thousand miles per hour or twenty-five thousand miles per day or nine million miles per year, none of us tumbles into orbit.

As you stand . . . observing God's workshop, let me pose a few questions. If he is able to place the stars in their sockets and suspend the sky like a curtain, do you think it is remotely possible that God is able to guide your life? If your God is mighty enough to ignite the sun, could it be that he is mighty enough to light your path? If he cares enough about the planet Saturn to give it rings or Venus to make it sparkle, is there an outside chance that he cares enough about you to meet your needs?

The Great House of God

February 19

Good Habits

So let us go on to grown-up teaching. Let us not go back over the beginning lessons we learned about Christ.

Hebrews 6:1

I like the story of the little boy who fell out of bed. When his mom asked him what happened, he answered, "I don't know. I guess I stayed too close to where I got in."

Easy to do the same with our faith. It's tempting just to stay where we got in and never move.

Pick a time in the not-too-distant past. A year or two ago. Now ask yourself a few questions. How does your prayer life today compare with then? How about your giving? Have both the amount and the joy increased? What about your church loyalty? Can you tell you've grown? And Bible study? Are you learning to learn?

Don't make the mistake of the little boy. Don't stay too close to where you got in. It's risky resting on the edge.

When God Whispers Your Name

February 20

Prayers Make a Difference

"We all know that God does not listen to sinners, but he listens to anyone who worships and obeys him."

John 9:31

Most of our prayer lives could use a tune-up.

Some prayer lives lack consistency. They're either a desert or an oasis. Long, arid dry spells interrupted by brief plunges into the waters of communion . . .

Others of us need sincerity. Our prayers are a bit hollow, memorized, and rigid. More liturgy than life. And though they are daily, they are dull.

Still others lack, well, honesty. We honestly wonder if prayer makes a difference. Why on earth would God in heaven want to talk to me? If God knows all, who am I to tell him anything? If God controls all, who am I to do anything?

Our prayers may be awkward. Our attempts may be feeble. But since the power of prayer is in the one who hears it and not the one who says it, our prayers do make a difference.

He Still Moves Stones

February 21

Beyond Imagination

"There are many rooms in my Father's house; . . .
I am going there to prepare a place for you."

John 14:2

Rest on this earth is a false rest. Beware of those who urge you to find happiness here; you won't find it. Guard against the false physicians who promise that joy is only a diet away, a marriage away, a job away, or a transfer away.

Try this. Imagine a perfect world. Whatever that means to you, imagine it. Does that mean peace? Then envision absolute tranquility. Does a perfect world imply joy? Then create your highest happiness. Will a perfect world have love? If so, ponder a place where love has no bounds. Whatever heaven means to you, imagine it. Get it firmly fixed in your mind.

And then smile as the Father reminds you, No one has ever imagined what God has prepared for those who love him.

When it comes to describing heaven, we are all happy failures.

When God Whispers Your Name

February 22

Changed to His Likeness

We Christians actually do have within us a portion of the very thoughts and mind of Christ.

1 Corinthians 2:16 TLB

The distance between our hearts and [Jesus' heart] seems so immense. How could we ever hope to have the heart of Jesus?

Ready for a surprise? You already do. . . . If you are in Christ, you already have the heart of Christ. One of the supreme yet unrealized promises of God is simply this: if you have given your life to Jesus, Jesus has given himself to you. He has made your heart his home. It would be hard to say it more succinctly than Paul does: "Christ lives in me" (Galatians 2:20 MSG).

He has moved in and unpacked his bags and is ready to change you "into his likeness from one degree of glory to another" (2 Corinthians 3:18 RSV).

Just Like Jesus

February 23

God's Help Is Near

Faith means being sure of the things we hope for and knowing that something is real even if we do not see it.

Hebrews 11:1

Faith is the belief that God is real and that God is good. It is a choice to believe that the one who made it all hasn't left it all and that he still sends light into the shadows and responds to gestures of faith.

Faith is the belief that God will do what is right.

God says that the more hopeless your circumstances, the more likely your salvation. The greater your cares, the more genuine your prayers. The darker the room, the greater the need for light.

God's help is near and always available, but it is only given to those who seek it.

He Still Moves Stones

February 24

A Cut Above

Be still, and know that I am God.

Psalm 46:10 NIV

The word *holy* means "to separate." The ancestry of the term can be traced back to an ancient word which means "to cut." To be holy, then, is to be a cut above the norm, superior, extraordinary. . . . The Holy One dwells on a different level from the rest of us. What frightens us does not frighten him. What troubles us does not trouble him.

I'm more a landlubber than a sailor, but I've puttered around in a bass boat enough to know the secret for finding land in a storm: You don't aim at another boat. You certainly don't stare at the waves. You set your sights on an object unaffected by the wind—a light on the shore—and go straight toward it.

When you set your sights on our God, you focus on one "a cut above" any storm life may bring. You find peace.

The Great House of God

February 25

Come and See

Nathanael said to Philip, "Can anything good come from Nazareth?" Philip answered, "Come and see."

John 1:46

Nathanael's question still lingers, even two thousand years later: "Can anything good come out of Nazareth?" Come and see.

Come and see the changed lives:

the alcoholic now dry,
the embittered now joyful,
the shamed now forgiven . . .
marriages rebuilt, the orphans embraced,
the imprisoned inspired.

Come and see the pierced hand of God touch the most common heart, wipe the tear from the wrinkled face, and forgive the ugliest sin.

Come and see. He avoids no seeker. He ignores no probe. He fears no search. Come and see.

A Gentle Thunder

February 26

God's Goodness

The rich and the poor are alike in that the Lord made them all.

Proverbs 22:2

Have you noticed that God doesn't ask you to prove that you will put your salary to good use? Have you noticed that God doesn't turn off your oxygen supply when you misuse his gifts? Aren't you glad that God doesn't give you only that which you remember to thank him for?

God's goodness is spurred by his nature, not by our worthiness.

Someone asked an associate of mine, "What biblical precedent do we have to help the poor who have no desire to become Christians?"

My friend responded with one word: "God."

God does it daily, for millions of people.

In the Eye of the Storm

February 27

What God Has Done

You have been saved by God's grace.

Ephesians 2:5

Read slowly and carefully Paul's description of what God has done for you: "When you were spiritually dead because of your sins and because you were not free from the power of your sinful self, God made you alive with Christ, and he forgave all our sins. He canceled the debt, which listed all the rules we failed to follow. He took away that record with its rules and nailed it to the cross. God stripped the spiritual rulers and powers of their authority. With the cross, he won the victory and showed the world that they were powerless" (Colossians 2:13–15).

As you look at the words above, answer this question. Who is doing the work? You or God? Who is active? You or God? Who is doing the saving? You or God?

He Still Moves Stones

February 28

Godless Living

Their thinking became useless. Their foolish minds were filled with darkness. They said they were wise, but they became fools.

Romans 1:21–22

Since the hedonist has never seen the hand who made the universe, he assumes there is no life beyond the here and now. He believes there is no truth beyond this room. No purpose beyond his own pleasure. No divine factor. He has no concern for the eternal.

The hedonist says, "Who cares? I may be bad, but so what? What I do is my business." He's more concerned about satisfying his passions than in knowing the Father. His life is so desperate for pleasure that he has no time or room for God.

Is he right? Is it okay to spend our days thumbing our noses at God and living it up?

Paul says, "Absolutely not!"

According to Romans 1, we lose more than stained-glass windows when we dismiss God. We lose our standard, our purpose, and our worship.

In the Grip of Grace

MARCH

Depend on the LORD; trust him, and he will take care of you.

—PSALM 37:5

March 1

Only One Thing Counts

No one has ever imagined what God has prepared for those who love him.

1 Corinthians 2:9

Think about the day Christ comes. There you are in the great circle of the redeemed. . . . Though you are one of a throng, it's as if you and Jesus are all alone.

I'm speculating now, but I wonder if Christ might say these words to you: "I'm so proud that you let me use you. Because of you, others are here today. Would you like to meet them?"

At that point Jesus might turn to the crowd and invite them. . . . One by one, they begin to step out and walk forward.

The first is your neighbor, a crusty old sort who lived next door. To be frank, you didn't expect to see him. "You never knew I was watching," he explains, "but I was. And because of you, I am here."

It's not long before you and your Savior are encircled by the delightful collection of souls you've touched. Some you know, most you don't, but for each you feel the same. You feel what Paul felt: "I'm so proud of your faith" (1 Thessalonians 2:19).

When Christ Comes

March 2

Live a Holy Life

"You should be a light for other people. Live so that they will see the good things you do and will praise your Father in heaven."

Matthew 5:16

You want to make a difference in your world? Live a holy life:

Be faithful to your spouse.
Be the one at the office who refuses to cheat.
Be the neighbor who acts neighborly.
Be the employee who does the work and doesn't complain.
Pay your bills.
Do your part and enjoy life.
Don't speak one message and live another.

People are watching the way we act more than they are listening to what we say.

A Gentle Thunder

March 3

Boldness Before the Throne

Let us, then, feel very sure that we can come before God's throne where there is grace.

Hebrews 4:16

Jesus tells us, "When you pray, pray like this. 'Our Father who is in heaven, hallowed be thy name. Thy kingdom come'" (Matthew 6:9–10).

When you say, "Thy kingdom come," you are inviting the Messiah himself to walk into your world. "Come, my King! Take your throne in our land. Be present in my heart. Be present in my office. Come into my marriage. Be Lord of my family, my fears, and my doubts." This is no feeble request; it's a bold appeal for God to occupy every corner of your life.

Who are you to ask such a thing? Who are you to ask God to take control of your world? You are his child, for heaven's sake! And so you ask boldly.

The Great House of God

March 4

Removing Doubt

"Who is more important: the one sitting at the table or the one serving? You think the one at the table is more important, but I am like a servant among you."

Luke 22:27

In Jesus' day the washing of feet was a task reserved not just for servants but for the lowest of servants. Every circle has its pecking order, and the circle of household workers was no exception. The servant at the bottom of the totem pole was expected to be the one on his knees with the towel and basin.

In this case the one with the towel and basin is the King of the universe. Hands that shaped the stars now wash away filth. Fingers that formed mountains now massage toes. And the one before whom all nations will one day kneel now kneels before his disciples. Hours before his own death, Jesus' concern is singular. He wants his disciples to know how much he loves them. More than removing dirt, Jesus is removing doubt.

Just Like Jesus

March 5

Sole Provider, Sole Comforter

"Come to me, all of you who are tired and have heavy loads, and I will give you rest."

Matthew 11:28

As long as Jesus is one of many options, he is no option.

As long as you can carry your burdens alone, you don't need a burden bearer. As long as your situation brings you no grief, you will receive no comfort. And as long as you can take him or leave him, you might as well leave him, because he won't be taken halfheartedly.

But when you mourn, when you get to the point of sorrow for your sins, when you admit that you have no other option but to cast all your cares on him, and when there is truly no other name that you can call, then cast all your cares on him, for he is waiting in the midst of the storm.

The Applause of Heaven

March 6

The Cost of His Gift

[Jesus] was not guilty, but he suffered for those who are guilty to bring you to God.

1 Peter 3:18

Christ came to earth for one reason: to give his life as a ransom for you, for me, for all of us. He sacrificed himself to give us a second chance. He would have gone to any lengths to do so. And he did. He went to the cross, where man's utter despair collided with God's unbending grace. And in that moment when God's great gift was complete, the compassionate Christ showed the world the cost of his gift.

He who was perfect gave that perfect record to us, and our imperfect record was given to him. As a result, God's holiness is honored and his children are forgiven.

The Applause of Heaven

March 7

Just in Time

May the God you serve all the time save you!

Daniel 6:16

Look at Jonah in the fish belly—surrounded by gastric juices and sucked-in seaweed. He prays. Before he can say amen, the belly convulses, the fish belches, and Jonah lands face first on the beach.

Look at Daniel in the lions' den; his prospects aren't much better than Jonah's. Jonah had been swallowed, and Daniel is about to be.

Or look at Joseph in the pit, a chalky hole in a hot desert. The lid has been pulled over the top and the wool has been pulled over his eyes. Like Jonah and Daniel, Joseph is trapped. He is out of options. There is no exit. There is no hope. Though the road to the palace takes a detour through a prison, it eventually ends up at the throne.

Such are the stories in the Bible. One near-death experience after another. Just when the neck is on the chopping block, just when the noose is around the neck, Calvary comes.

He Still Moves Stones

March 8

Led by the Spirit

The true children of God are those who let God's Spirit lead them.

Romans 8:14

To hear many of us talk, you'd think we didn't believe that verse. You'd think we didn't believe in the Trinity. We talk about the Father and study the Son—but when it comes to the Holy Spirit, we are confused at best and frightened at worst. Confused because we've never been taught. Frightened because we've been taught to be afraid.

May I simplify things a bit? The Holy Spirit is the presence of God in our lives, carrying on the work of Jesus. The Holy Spirit helps us in three directions—inwardly (by granting us the fruits of the Spirit, Galatians 5:22–24), upwardly (by praying for us, Romans 8:26) and outwardly (by pouring God's love into our hearts, Romans 5:5).

When God Whispers Your Name

March 9

God's Will . . . Be Done

"May your kingdom come and what you want be done, here on earth as it is in heaven."

Matthew 6:10

To pray, "Thy will be done" is to seek the heart of God. The word *will* means "strong desire." . . . [So] what is his heart? His passion? He wants you to know it.

Shall God hide from us what he is going to do? Apparently not, for he has gone to great lengths to reveal his will to us. Could he have done more than send his Son to lead us? Could he have done more than give his Word to teach us? Could he have done more than orchestrate events to awaken us? Could he have done more than send his Holy Spirit to counsel us?

God is not the God of confusion, and wherever he sees sincere seekers with confused hearts, you can bet your sweet December that he will do whatever it takes to help them see his will.

The Great House of God

March 10

God Is Crazy About You

"God even knows how many hairs are on your head."

Matthew 10:30

There are many reasons God saves you: to bring glory to himself, to appease his justice, to demonstrate his sovereignty. But one of the sweetest reasons God saved you is because he is fond of you. He likes having you around. He thinks you are the best thing to come down the pike in quite a while.

If God had a refrigerator, your picture would be on it. If he had a wallet, your photo would be in it. He sends you flowers every spring and a sunrise every morning. Whenever you want to talk, he'll listen. He can live anywhere in the universe, and he chose your heart.

Face it, friend. He's crazy about you.

A Gentle Thunder

March 11

Behold His Mercy!

Be kind and loving to each other, and forgive each other just as God forgave you in Christ.

Ephesians 4:32

Jesus wraps a servant's girdle around his waist, takes up the basin, and kneels before one of the disciples. He unlaces a sandal and gently lifts the foot and places it in the basin, covers it with water, and begins to bathe it. One by one, one grimy foot after another, Jesus works his way down the row.

You can be sure Jesus knows the future of these feet he is washing. These twenty-four feet will not spend the next day following their master, defending his cause. These feet will dash for cover at the flash of a Roman sword. Only one pair of feet won't abandon him in the garden. One disciple won't desert him at Gethsemane—Judas won't even make it that far!

Behold the gift Jesus gives his followers! He knows what these men are about to do . . . and when they do, he wants them to remember how his knees knelt before them and he washed their feet. He wants them to realize those feet are still clean. He forgave their sin before they even committed it. He offered mercy before they even sought it.

Just Like Jesus

March 12
Slaves to Goodness

Now you are free from sin and have become slaves of God. This brings you a life that is only for God, and this gives you life forever.

Romans 6:22

How could we who have been freed from sin return to it? Before Christ our lives were out of control, sloppy, and indulgent. We didn't even know we were slobs until we met him.

Then he moved in. Things began to change. What we threw around we began putting away. What we neglected we cleaned up. What had been clutter became order. Oh, there were and still are occasional lapses of thought and deed, but by and large he got our house in order.

Suddenly we find ourselves wanting to do good. Go back to the old mess? Are you kidding? "In the past you were slaves to sin—sin controlled you. But thank God, you fully obeyed the things that you were taught. You were made free from sin, and now you are slaves to goodness" (Romans 6:17–18).

In the Grip of Grace

March 13

A Burst of Love

"Seek God's kingdom, and all the other things you need will be given to you."

Luke 12:31

Sometimes God is so touched by what he sees that he gives us what we need and not simply that for which we ask.

It's a good thing. For who would have ever thought to ask God for what he gives? Which of us would have dared to say, "God, would you please hang yourself on a tool of torture as a substitution for every mistake I have ever committed?" And then have the audacity to add, "And after you forgive me, could you prepare me a place in your house to live forever?"

And if that wasn't enough: "And would you please live within me and protect me and guide me and bless me with more than I could ever deserve?"

Honestly, would we have the chutzpah to ask for that?

Jesus already knows the cost of grace. He already knows the price of forgiveness. But he offers it anyway. Love burst his heart.

He Still Moves Stones

March 14

Heaven's on Your Side

The One who died for us . . . is in the presence of God at this very moment sticking up for us.

Romans 8:34 MSG

Jesus is praying for us. Jesus has spoken and Satan has listened. The devil may land a punch or two. He may even win a few rounds, but he never wins the fight. Why? Because Jesus takes up for you. "He is able always to save those who come to God through him because he always lives, asking God to help them" (Hebrews 7:25).

Jesus, at this very moment, is protecting you. Evil must pass through Christ before it can touch you. And God will "never let you be pushed past your limit; he'll always be there to help you come through it" (1 Corinthians 10:13 MSG).

When Christ Comes

March 15

The Fire Within

Jesus began to explain everything that had been written about himself in the Scriptures.

Luke 24:27

When [the disciples] saw who he was, he disappeared. They said to each other, 'It felt like a fire burning in us when Jesus talked to us on the road and explained the Scriptures to us'" (Luke 24:31–32).

Don't you love that verse? They knew they had been with Jesus because of the fire within them. God reveals his will by setting a torch to your soul. He gave Jeremiah a fire for hard hearts. He gave Nehemiah a fire for a forgotten city. He set Abraham on fire for a land he'd never seen. He set Isaiah on fire with a vision he couldn't resist. Forty years of fruitless preaching didn't extinguish the fire of Noah.

Mark it down: Jesus comes to set you on fire! He walks as a torch from heart to heart, warming the cold and thawing the chilled and stirring the ashes. He comes to purge infection and illuminate your direction.

The Great House of God

March 16

Listen for His Voice

"Never will I leave you; never will I forsake you."

Hebrews 13:5 niv

Let me state something important. There is never a time during which Jesus is not speaking. Never. There is never a place in which Jesus is not present. Never. There is never a room so dark . . . a lounge so sensual . . . an office so sophisticated . . . that the ever-present, ever-pursuing, relentlessly tender Friend is not there, tapping gently on the doors of our hearts—waiting to be invited in.

Few hear his voice. Fewer still open the door.

But never interpret our numbness as his absence. For amidst the fleeting promises of pleasure is the timeless promise of his presence.

"Surely I am with you always, to the very end of the age" (Matthew 28:20 niv).

There is no chorus so loud that the voice of God cannot be heard . . . if we will but listen.

In the Eye of the Storm

March 17

Because of His Gift

I want to know Christ and the power that raised him from the dead. I want to share in his sufferings and become like him in his death.

Philippians 3:10

Trace the path of this Savior, the God who swapped heavenly royalty for earthly poverty. His bed became, at best, a borrowed pallet—and usually the hard earth. He was dependent on handouts for his income. He was sometimes so hungry he would eat raw grain or pick fruit off a tree. He knew what it meant to have no home. He was ridiculed. His neighbors tried to lynch him. Some called him a lunatic. His family tried to confine him to their house. His friends weren't always faithful to him.

He was accused of a crime he never committed. Witnesses were hired to lie. The jury was rigged. A judge swayed by politics handed down the death penalty.

They killed him.

And why? Because of the gift that only he could give.

The Applause of Heaven

March 18

Doing What's Right

This is the victory that conquers the world—our faith.

1 John 5:4

You get impatient with your own life, trying to master a habit or control a sin—and in your frustration begin to wonder where the power of God is. Be patient. God is using today's difficulties to strengthen you for tomorrow. He is *equipping* you. The God who makes things grow will help you bear fruit.

Dwell on the fact that God lives within you. Think about the power that gives you life. The realization that God is dwelling within you may change the places you want to go and the things you want to do today.

Do what is right this week, whatever it is, whatever comes down the path, whatever problems and dilemmas you face—just do what's right. Maybe no one else is doing what's right, but you do what's right. You be honest. You take a stand. You be true. After all, regardless of what you do, God does what is right: he saves you with his grace.

Walking with the Savior

March 19

The Basin of God's Grace

The blood of Jesus, God's Son, cleanses us from every sin.

1 John 1:7

John tells us, "We are *being cleansed* from every sin by the blood of Jesus (emphasis added)." In other words, we are *always being cleansed.* The cleansing is not a promise for the future but a reality in the present. Let a speck of dust fall on the soul of a saint, and it is washed away. Let a spot of filth land on the heart of God's child, and the filth is wiped away.

Our Savior kneels down and gazes upon the darkest acts of our lives. But rather than recoil in horror, he reaches out in kindness and says, "I can clean that if you want." And from the basin of his grace, he scoops a palm full of mercy and washes away our sin.

But that's not all he does. Because he lives in us, you and I can do the same. Because he has forgiven us, we can forgive others.

Just Like Jesus

March 20

From Heaven Itself

God . . . forgave all your sins. He canceled the debt, which listed all the rules we failed to follow.

Colossians 2:13–14

All the world religions can be placed in one of two camps: legalism or grace. Humankind does it or God does it. Salvation as a wage based on deeds done—or salvation as a gift based on Christ's death.

A legalist believes the supreme force behind salvation is you. If you look right, speak right, and belong to the right segment of the right group, you will be saved. The brunt of responsibility doesn't lie within God; it lies within you.

The result? The outside sparkles. The talk is good and the step is true. But look closely. Listen carefully. Something is missing. What is it? Joy. What's there? Fear. (That you won't do enough.) Arrogance. (That you have done enough.) Failure. (That you have made a mistake.)

Spiritual life is not a human endeavor. It is rooted in and orchestrated by the Holy Spirit. Every spiritual achievement is created and energized by God.

He Still Moves Stones

March 21

God Hears Our Prayers

The Lord hears good people when they cry out to him, and he saves them from all their troubles.

Psalm 34:17

When [a friend] tells Jesus of the illness [of Lazarus], he says, "Lord, the one you love is sick." He doesn't base his appeal on the imperfect love of the one in need, but on the perfect love of the Savior. He doesn't say, "The one *who loves you* is sick." He says, "The one you love is sick." The power of the prayer, in other words, does not depend on the one who makes the prayer, but on the one who hears the prayer.

We can and must repeat the phrase in manifold ways. "The one you love is tired, sad, hungry, lonely, fearful, depressed." The words of the prayer vary, but the response never changes. The Savior hears the prayer. He silences heaven, so he won't miss a word. He hears the prayer.

The Great House of God

March 22

Dark Nights—God's Light

Pray for all people, asking God for what they need and being thankful to him.

1 Timothy 2:1

You wonder if it is a blessing or a curse to have a mind that never rests. But you would rather be a cynic than a hypocrite, so you continue to pray with one eye open and wonder . . .

about starving children
about Christians in cancer wards.

Tough questions. Throw-in-the-towel questions. Questions the disciples must have asked in the storm.

All they could see were black skies as they bounced in the battered boat.

[Then] a figure came to them walking on the water. It wasn't what they expected. They almost missed seeing the answer to their prayers.

And unless we look and listen closely, we risk making the same mistake. God's lights in our dark nights are as numerous as the stars, if only we'll look for them.

In the Eye of the Storm

March 23

The Cloak of Humanity

Jesus took Peter, James, and John with him, and he began to be very sad and troubled.

Mark 14:33

During the days of Jesus' life on earth, he offered up prayers and petitions with *loud cries and tears* to the one who could save him from death" (Hebrews 5:7 NIV; emphasis mine).

My, what a portrait! Jesus is in pain. Jesus is on the stage of fear. Jesus is cloaked, not in sainthood, but in humanity.

The next time the fog finds you, you might do well to remember Jesus in the garden. The next time you think that no one understands, reread the fourteenth chapter of Mark. The next time your self-pity convinces you that no one cares, pay a visit to Gethsemane. And the next time you wonder if God really perceives the pain that prevails on this dusty planet, listen to him pleading among the twisted trees.

No Wonder They Call Him the Savior

March 24

The Standard

We are made holy through the sacrifice Christ made in his body once and for all time.

Hebrews 10:10

Only the holy will see God. Holiness is a prerequisite to heaven. Perfection is a requirement for eternity. We wish it weren't so. We act like it isn't so. We act like those who are "decent" will see God. We suggest that those who try hard will see God. We act as if we're good if we never do anything too bad. And that goodness is enough to qualify us for heaven.

Sounds right to us, but it doesn't sound right to God. And he sets the standard. And the standard is high: "You must be perfect, just as your Father in heaven is perfect" (Matthew 5:48).

You see, in God's plan, God is the standard for perfection. We don't compare ourselves to others; they are just as fouled up as we are. The goal is to be like him; anything less is inadequate.

He Still Moves Stones

March 25

A Few More Scenes

"In [this] world you will have tribulation; but be of good cheer, I have overcome the world."

John 16:33 NKJV

God has kept no secrets. He has told us that, while on this yellow brick road [of life], we will experience trouble. Disease will afflict bodies. Divorce will break hearts. Death will make widows and devastation will destroy countries. We should not expect any less. But just because the devil shows up and cackles, we needn't panic.

Our Master speaks of an accomplished deed, "It is finished" (John 19:30). The battle is over. Be alert. But don't be alarmed. . . . The manuscript has been published. The book has been bound. Satan is loosed for a season, but the season is oh-so-brief. Just a few more scenes, just a few more turns in the road, and his end will come.

When Christ Comes

March 26

A Godly Touch

Jesus reached out his hand and touched the man and said, "I will. Be healed!"

Matthew 8:3

Oh, the power of a godly touch. Haven't you known it? The doctor who treated you, or the teacher who dried your tears? Was there a hand holding yours at a funeral? Another on your shoulder during a trial? A handshake of welcome at a new job?

Can't we offer the same?

Many of you already do. Some of you have the master touch of the Physician himself. You use your hands to pray over the sick and minister to the weak. If you aren't touching them personally, your hands are writing letters, speed dialing, baking pies. You have learned the power of a touch.

But others of us tend to forget. Our hearts are good; it's just that our memories are bad. We forget how significant one touch can be.

Aren't we glad Jesus didn't make the same mistake?

Just Like Jesus

March 27

God's Priority

Depend on the Lord; trust him, and he will take care of you.

Psalm 37:5

God is committed to caring for our needs. Paul tells us that a man who won't feed his own family is worse than an unbeliever (1 Timothy 5:8). How much more will a holy God care for his children? After all, how can we fulfill his mission unless our needs are met? How can we teach or minister or influence unless we have our basic needs satisfied? Will God enlist us in his army and not provide a commissary? Of course not.

"I pray that the God of peace will give you everything you need so you can do what he wants" (Hebrews 13:20). Hasn't that prayer been answered in our life? We may not have had a feast, but haven't we always had food? Perhaps there was no banquet, but at least there was bread. And many times there was a banquet.

The Great House of God

March 28

God's Child

The Father has loved us so much that we are called children of God. And we really are his children.

1 John 3:1

Let me tell you who you are. In fact, let me proclaim who you are.

You are an heir of God and a co-heir with Christ (Romans 8:17 NKJV).

You are eternal, like an angel (Luke 20:36).

You have a crown that will last forever (1 Corinthians 9:25).

You are a holy priest (1 Peter 2:5), a treasured possession (Exodus 19:5). . . .

But more than any of the above—more significant than any title or position—is the simple fact that you are God's child.

"We really are his children."

As a result, if something is important to you, it's important to God.

He Still Moves Stones

March 29

Footprints of Discipleship

"All people will know that you are my followers if you love each other."

John 13:35

Watch a small boy follow his dad through the snow. He stretches to step where his dad stepped. Not an easy task. His small legs extend as far as they can so his feet can fall in his father's prints.

The father, seeing what the son is doing, smiles and begins taking shorter steps, so the son can follow.

It's a picture of discipleship.

In our faith we follow in someone's steps. A parent, a teacher, a hero—none of us is the first to walk the trail. All of us have someone we follow.

In our faith we leave footprints to guide others. A child, a friend, a recent convert. None should be left to walk the trail alone.

It's the principle of discipleship.

The Inspirational Study Bible

March 30

One Incredible Plan

He humbled himself and was fully obedient to God, even when that caused his death—death on a cross.

Philippians 2:8

When human hands fastened the divine hands to a cross with spikes, it wasn't the soldiers who held the hands of Jesus steady. It was God who held them steady. Those same hands that formed the oceans and built the mountains. Those same hands that designed the dawn and crafted each cloud. Those same hands that blueprinted one incredible plan for you and me.

Take a stroll out to the hill. Out to Calvary. Out to the cross where, with holy blood, the hand that placed you on the planet wrote the promise, "God would give up his only Son before he'd give up on you."

Six Hours One Friday

March 31

THE SHEPHERD'S VOICE

A time is coming when all who are in their graves will hear his voice and come out—those who have done good will rise to live. . . .

JOHN 5:28–29 NIV

A DAY IS COMING WHEN EVERYONE WILL HEAR [Jesus'] voice. A day is coming when all the other voices will be silenced; his voice—and his voice only—will be heard.

Some will hear his voice for the very first time. It's not that he never spoke; it's just that they never listened. For these, God's voice will be the voice of a stranger. They will hear it once—and never hear it again. They will spend eternity fending off the voices they followed on earth.

But others will be called from their graves by a familiar voice. For they are sheep who know their shepherd. They are servants who opened the door when Jesus knocked.

Now the door will open again. Only this time, it won't be Jesus who walks into our house; it will be we who walk into his.

IN THE EYE OF THE STORM

APRIL

Be strong in the Lord and in his great power.

—Ephesians 6:10

April 1
A Meeting of Moments

[They] put him to death by nailing him to a cross. But this was God's plan which he had made long ago.

Acts 2:23

The cross was no accident.

Jesus' death was not the result of a panicking cosmological engineer. The cross wasn't a tragic surprise. Calvary was not a knee-jerk response to a world plummeting toward destruction. It wasn't a patch-up job or a stop-gap measure. The death of the Son of God was anything but an unexpected peril.

No, it was part of an incredible plan. A calculated choice.

The moment the forbidden fruit touched the lips of Eve, the shadow of a cross appeared on the horizon. And between that moment and the moment the man with the mallet placed the spike against the wrist of God, a master plan was fulfilled.

God Came Near

April 2

A Cross-Shaped Shadow

John said, "Look, the Lamb of God, who takes away the sin of the world!"

John 1:29

Jesus was born crucified. Whenever he became conscious of who he was, he also became conscious of what he had to do. The cross-shaped shadow could always be seen. And the screams of hell's imprisoned could always be heard.

This explains the glint of determination on his face as he turned to go to Jerusalem for the last time. He was on his death march (Luke 9:51).

This explains the resoluteness in the words "The reason my Father loves me is that I lay down my life—only to take it up again. No one takes it from me, but I lay it down of my own accord" (John 10:17–18 niv).

So call it what you wish: An act of grace. A plan of redemption. A martyr's sacrifice. But whatever you call it, don't call it an accident. It was anything but that.

God Came Near

April 3

You Were in His Prayers

Then Jesus went about a stone's throw away from them. He kneeled down and prayed.

Luke 22:41

The final prayer of Jesus was about you. His final pain was for you. His final passion was for you. Before he went to the cross, Jesus went to the garden. And when he spoke with his Father, you were in his prayers.

And God couldn't turn his back on you. He couldn't because he saw you, and one look at you was all it took to convince him. Right there in the middle of a world that isn't fair. He saw you cast into a river of life you didn't request. He saw you betrayed by those you love. He saw you with a body which gets sick and a heart which grows weak.

On the eve of the cross, Jesus made his decision. He would rather go to hell for you than go to heaven without you.

And the Angels Were Silent

April 4

The Debt Is Paid

Though your sins are like scarlet, they can be as white as snow.
Though your sins are deep red, they can be white like wool.

Isaiah 1:18

When Jesus told us to pray for forgiveness of our debts as we forgive our own debtors, he knew who would be the one to pay the debt. As he would hang on the cross, he would say, "It is finished" . . . the debt is paid!

There are some facts that will never change. One fact is that you are forgiven. If you are in Christ, when he sees you, your sins are covered—he doesn't see them. He sees you better than you see yourself. And that is a glorious fact of your life.

Walking with the Savior

April 5

The Worshipful Heart

Come, let's worship him and bow down. Let's kneel before the Lord who made us.

Psalm 95:6

Worship. In two thousand years we haven't worked out the kinks. We still struggle for the right words in prayer. We still fumble over Scripture. We don't know when to kneel. We don't know when to stand. We don't know how to pray.

Worship is a daunting task.

For that reason, God gave us the Psalms—a praise book for God's people. . . . This collection of hymns and petitions are strung together by one thread—a heart hungry for God.

Some are defiant. Others are reverent. Some are to be sung. Others are to be prayed. Some are intensely personal. Others are written as if the whole world would use them.

The very variety should remind us that worship is personal. No secret formula exists. What moves you may stymie another. Each worships differently. But each should worship.

The Inspirational Study Bible

April 6

Heaven's Solution

"I pray these things while I am still in the world so that these followers can have all of my joy in them."

John 17:13

What Jesus dreamed of doing and what he seemed able to do were separated by an impossible gulf. So Jesus prayed.

We don't know what he prayed about. But I have my guesses. He prayed for the impossible to happen.

Or maybe I'm wrong. Maybe he didn't ask for anything. Maybe he just stood quietly in the presence of Presence and basked in the Majesty. Perhaps he placed his war-weary self before the throne and rested.

Maybe he lifted his head out of the confusion of earth long enough to hear the solution of heaven. Perhaps he was reminded that hard hearts don't faze the Father. That problem people don't perturb the Eternal One.

In the Eye of the Storm

April 7

One Word from His Lips

"I have given you power . . . that is greater than the enemy has. "

Luke 10:19

Many players appear on the stage of Gethsemane. Judas and his betrayal. Peter and his sword. The soldiers and their weapons. And though these are crucial, they aren't instrumental. The encounter is not between Jesus and the soldiers; it is between God and Satan. Satan dares to enter yet another garden, but God stands and Satan hasn't a prayer.

Satan falls in the presence of Christ. One word from his lips, and the finest army in the world collapsed.

Satan is silent in the proclamation of Christ. Not once did the enemy speak without Jesus' invitation. Before Christ, Satan has nothing to say.

Satan is powerless against the protection of Christ.

When Jesus says he will keep you safe, he means it. Hell will have to get through him to get to you. Jesus is able to protect you. When he says he will get you home, he will get you home.

A Gentle Thunder

April 8

Faith Sees the Savior

Be strong in the Lord and in his great power.

Ephesians 6:10

I stand a few feet from a mirror and see the face of a man who failed, who failed his Maker. Again. I promised I wouldn't, but I did. I was quiet when I should have been bold. I took a seat when I should have taken a stand.

If this were the first time, it would be different. But it isn't. How many times can one fall and expect to be caught?

Your eyes look in the mirror and see a sinner, a failure, a promise-breaker. But by faith you look in the mirror and see a robed prodigal bearing the ring of grace on your finger and the kiss of your Father on your face.

Your eyes see your faults. Your faith sees your Savior.

Your eyes see your guilt. Your faith sees his blood.

When God Whispers Your Name

April 9

Tipped Scales

Christ's love is greater than anyone can ever know, but I pray that you will be able to know that love.

Ephesians 3:19

It wasn't right that spikes pierced the hands that formed the earth. And it wasn't right that the Son of God was forced to hear the silence of God.

It wasn't right, but it happened.

For while Jesus was on the cross, God sat on his hands. He turned his back. He ignored the screams of the innocent.

He sat in silence while the sins of the world were placed upon his Son. And he did nothing while a cry a million times bloodier than John's echoed in the black sky: "My God, my God, why have you forsaken me?"

Was it right? No.

Was it fair? No.

Was it love? Yes.

The Applause of Heaven

April 10

His Broken Heart

When he saw the crowds, he felt sorry for them because they were hurting and helpless, like sheep without a shepherd.

Matthew 9:36

I can't understand it. I honestly cannot. Why did Jesus [die on the cross]? Oh, I know, I know. I have heard the official answers. "To gratify the old law." "To fulfill prophecy." And these answers are right. They are. But there is something more here. Something very compassionate. Something yearning. Something personal.

What is it?

Could it be that his heart was broken for all the people who cast despairing eyes toward the dark heavens and cry the same "Why?" Could it be that his heart was broken for the hurting?

I imagine him bending close to those who hurt. I imagine him listening. I picture his eyes misting and a pierced hand brushing away a tear. He who also was once alone, understands.

No Wonder They Call Him the Savior

April 11

Love Hung on a Cross

"God loved the world so much that he gave his one and only Son so that whoever believes in him may not be lost, but have eternal life."

John 3:16

He looked around the hill and foresaw a scene. Three figures hung on three crosses. Arms spread. Heads fallen forward. They moaned with the wind.

Men clad in soldier's garb sat on the ground near the trio.

Women clad in sorrow huddled at the foot of the hill, their faces tear-streaked.

All heaven stood to fight. All nature rose to rescue. All eternity poised to protect. But the Creator gave no command.

"It must be done . . ." he said, and withdrew.

The angel spoke again. "It would be less painful . . ."

The Creator interrupted softly. "But it wouldn't be love."

In the Eye of the Storm

April 12

The Message of God to Man

When Jesus tasted the vinegar, he said, "It is finished." Then he bowed his head and died.

John 19:30

"It is finished."

Stop and listen a moment. Let the words wind through your heart. Imagine the cry from the cross. The sky is dark. The other two victims are moaning. Jeering mouths of the crowd are silent. Perhaps there is thunder. Perhaps there is weeping. Perhaps there is silence. Then Jesus draws in a deep breath, pushes his feet down on that Roman nail, and cries, "It is finished!"

What was finished?

The history-long plan of redeeming man was finished. The message of God to man was finished. The works done by Jesus as a man on earth were finished. The sting of death had been removed. It was over.

No Wonder They Call Him the Savior

April 13

The Key of Our Faith

Since Jesus died and broke loose from the grave, God will most certainly bring back to life those who died in Jesus.

1 Thessalonians 4:14 msg

For any follower of Christ, the promise is simply this: The resurrection of Jesus is proof and preview of our own.

But can we trust the promise? Is the resurrection a reality? Are the claims of the empty tomb true? This is not only a good question. It is *the* question. For as Paul wrote, "If Christ has not been raised, then your faith has nothing to it; you are still guilty of your sins" (1 Corinthians 15:17). In other words, if Christ has been raised, then his followers will join him; but if not, then his followers are fools. The resurrection, then, is the keystone in the arch of the Christian faith.

When Christ Comes

April 14

A Noble Motivation

At dawn on the first day, Mary Magdalene and another woman named Mary went to look at the tomb.

Matthew 28:1

It isn't hope that leads [Mary and Mary Magdalene] up the mountain to the tomb. It is duty. Naked devotion. They expect nothing in return. What could Jesus give? What could a dead man offer? The two women are not climbing the mountain to receive; they are going to the tomb to give. Period.

There is no motivation more noble.

Service prompted by duty. This is the call of discipleship.

He Still Moves Stones

April 15

A Holy Task

Everything you do or say should be done to obey Jesus your Lord.

Colossians 3:17

Mary and Mary [Magdalene] knew a task had to be done—Jesus' body had to be prepared for burial. Peter didn't offer to do it. Andrew didn't volunteer. So the two Marys decided to do it.

I wonder if halfway to the tomb they had sat down and reconsidered. What if they'd looked at each other and shrugged, "What's the use?" What if they had given up? What if one had thrown up her arms in frustration and bemoaned, "I'm tired of being the only one who cares. Let Andrew do something for a change. Let Nathaniel show some leadership."

Whether or not they were tempted to, I'm glad they didn't quit. That would have been tragic. You see, we know something they didn't. We know the Father was watching. Mary and Mary thought they were alone. They weren't. They thought their journey was unnoticed. They were wrong. God knew.

He Still Moves Stones

April 16

The Only Path

"I am the way, and the truth, and the life. The only way to the Father is through me."

John 14:6

Tolerance. A prized virtue today. The ability to be understanding of those with whom you differ is a sign of sophistication. Jesus, too, was a champion of tolerance:

- Tolerant of the disciples when they doubted
- Tolerant of the crowds when they misunderstood
- Tolerant of us when we fall

But there is one area where Jesus was intolerant. There was one area where he was unindulgent and dogmatic.

As far as he was concerned, when it comes to salvation, there aren't several roads. There is only one road. There aren't several paths. There is only one path. And that path is Jesus himself.

That is why it is so hard for people to believe in Jesus. It's much easier to consider him one of several options rather than the option. But such a philosophy is no option.

A Gentle Thunder

April 17

Insufficient Funds

People cannot do any work that will make them right with God.

Romans 4:5

If Christ had not covered us with his grace, each of us would be overdrawn on [our heavenly bank] account. When it comes to goodness, we would have insufficient funds. Inadequate holiness. God requires a certain balance of virtue in our account, and it's more than any of us has alone. Our holiness account shows insufficient funds, and only the holy will see the Lord; what can we do?

We could try making a few deposits. Maybe if I wave at my neighbor or compliment my husband or go to church next Sunday, I'll get caught up. But how do you know when you've made enough?

If you are trying to justify your own statement, forget ever having peace. . . . You are trying to justify an account you can't justify. "It is God who justifies" (Romans 8:33).

The Great House of God

April 18

Not Perfection, but Forgiveness

Christ had no sin, but God made him become sin so that in Christ we could become right with God.

2 Corinthians 5:21

It wasn't the Romans who nailed Jesus to the cross. It wasn't spikes that held Jesus to the cross. What held him to that cross was his conviction that it was necessary that he become sin—that he who is pure become sin and that the wrath of God be poured down, not upon the creation, but upon the Creator.

When the One who knew no sin became sin for us, when the sinless One was covered with all the sins of all the world, God didn't call his army of angels to save him. He didn't, because he knew he would rather give up his Son than give up on us.

Regardless of what you've done, it's not too late. Regardless of how far you've fallen, it's not too late. It doesn't matter how low the mistake is, it's not too late to dig down, pull out that mistake, and then let it go—and be free.

What makes a Christian a Christian is not perfection, but forgiveness.

Walking with the Savior

April 19

Whispered Wonderings

She will have a son, and they will name him Immanuel, which means "God is with us."

Matthew 1:23

The white space between Bible verses is fertile soil for questions. One can hardly read Scripture without whispering, "I wonder . . ."

"I wonder if Eve ever ate any more fruit."

"I wonder if Noah slept well during storms."

But in our wonderings, there is one question we never need to ask. Does God care? Do we matter to God? Does he still love his children?

Through the small face of the stable-born baby, he says yes.

Yes, your sins are forgiven.

Yes, your name is written in heaven.

And, yes, God has entered your world. Immanuel. God is with us.

He Still Moves Stones

April 20

The Fire of Your Heart

My God, I want to do what you want.
Your teachings are in my heart.

Psalm 40:8

Want to know God's will for your life? Then answer this question: What ignites your heart? Forgotten orphans? Untouched nations? The inner city? The outer limits?

Heed the fire within!

Do you have a passion to sing? Then sing! Are you stirred to manage? Then manage! Do you ache for the ill? Then treat them! Do you hurt for the lost? Then teach them!

As a young man, I felt the call to preach. Unsure if I was correct in my reading of God's will for me, I sought the counsel of a minister I admired. His counsel still rings true. "Don't preach," he said, "unless you have to."

As I pondered his words, I found my answer: "I have to. If I don't, the fire will consume me."

What is the fire that consumes you?

The Great House of God

April 21
A Cleared Calendar

Jesus often withdrew to lonely places and prayed.

Luke 5:16 niv

How long has it been since you let God have you? I mean really have you? How long since you gave him a portion of undiluted, uninterrupted time listening for his voice? Apparently, Jesus did. He made a deliberate effort to spend time with God.

Spend much time reading about the listening life of Jesus, and a distinct pattern emerges. He spent regular time with God, praying and listening. Mark says, "Very early in the morning, while it was still dark, Jesus got up, left the house and went off to a solitary place, where he prayed" (Mark 1:35 niv).

Let me ask the obvious. If Jesus, the Son of God, the sinless Savior of humankind, thought it worthwhile to clear his calendar to pray, wouldn't we be wise to do the same?

Just Like Jesus

April 22

God's Magnum Opus

We know that when Christ comes again, we will be like him, because we will see him as he really is.

1 John 3:2

When you arrive [in heaven] . . . something wonderful will happen. A final transformation will occur. You will be just like Jesus.

Of all the blessings of heaven, one of the greatest will be you! You will be God's magnum opus, his work of art. The angels will gasp. God's work will be completed. At last, you will have a heart like his.

You will love with a perfect love.
You will worship with a radiant face.
You'll hear each word God speaks.
Your heart will be pure, your words will be like jewels, your thoughts will be like treasures.
You will be just like Jesus. You will, at long last, have a heart like his.

Just Like Jesus

April 23

Friends with God

"I no longer call you servants, . . . but I call you friends."

John 15:15

Through Christ's sacrifice, our past is pardoned and our future secure. And "since we have been made right with God by our faith, we have peace with God" (Romans 5:1).

Peace with God. What a happy consequence of faith! Not just peace between countries, peace between neighbors, or peace at home; salvation brings peace with God.

God is no longer a foe, but a friend. We are at peace with him.

In the Grip of Grace

April 24

Confession Creates Peace

Happy is the person whose sins are forgiven,
whose wrongs are pardoned.

Psalm 32:1

If we are already forgiven, then why does Jesus teach us to pray, "Forgive us our debts"?

The very reason you would want your children to do the same. If my children violate one of my standards or disobey a rule, I don't disown them. I don't kick them out of the house or tell them to change their last name. But I do expect them to be honest and apologize. And until they do, the tenderness of our relationship will suffer. The nature of the relationship won't be altered, but the intimacy will.

The same happens in our walk with God. Confession does not create a relationship with God, it simply nourishes it. If you are a believer, admission of sins does not alter your position before God, but it does enhance your peace with God.

The Great House of God

April 25

Something Deep Within

The heavens declare the glory of God.

Psalm 19:1 niv

God's judgment [on the day Christ returns] is based upon humanity's response to the message received. He will never hold us accountable for what he doesn't tell us. At the same time, he will never let us die without telling us something. Even those who never heard of Christ are given a message about the character of God. "The heavens declare the glory of God" (Psalm 19:1 niv).

Nature is God's first missionary. Where there is no Bible, there are sparkling stars. Where there are no preachers, there are springtimes. . . . If a person has nothing but nature, then nature is enough to reveal something about God. As Paul says: "God's law is not something alien, imposed on us from without, but woven into the very fabric of our creation. There is something deep within [people] that echoes God's yes and no, right and wrong. Their response to God's yes and no will become public knowledge on the day God makes his final decision about every man and woman" (Romans 2:15–16 msg).

When Christ Comes

April 26

Character Creates Courage

All you who put your hope in the Lord be strong and brave.

Psalm 31:24

A legend from India tells about a mouse who was terrified of cats until a magician agreed to transform him into a cat. That resolved his fear . . . until he met a dog, so the magician changed him into a dog. The mouse-turned-cat-turned-dog was content until he met a tiger—so, once again, the magician changed him into what he feared. But when the tiger came complaining that he had met a hunter, the magician refused to help. "I will make you into a mouse again, for though you have the body of a tiger, you still have the heart of a mouse."

Sound familiar? How many people do you know who have built a formidable exterior, only to tremble inside with fear? We face our fears with force . . . or . . . we stockpile wealth. We seek security in things. We cultivate fame and seek status.

But do these approaches work?

Courage is an outgrowth of who we are. Exterior supports may temporarily sustain, but only inward character creates courage.

The Applause of Heaven

April 27

One-of-a-Kind

You made my whole being; you formed me in my mother's body.

Psalm 139:13

In my closet hangs a sweater that I seldom wear. It is too small.

I should throw that sweater away. But love won't let me.

It's the creation of a devoted mother expressing her love. Each strand was chosen with care. Each thread was selected with affection. It is valuable not because of its function, but because of its maker.

That must have been what the psalmist had in mind when he wrote, "You knit me together in my mother's womb" (niv).

Think on those words. You were knitted together. You aren't an accident. You weren't mass-produced. You aren't an assembly-line product.

You were deliberately planned, specifically gifted, and lovingly positioned on this earth by the Master Craftsman. In a system that ranks the value of a human by the figures of his salary or the shape of her legs . . . let me tell you something: Jesus' plan is a reason for joy!

The Applause of Heaven

April 28

Voice of Grace

"I tell you the truth, today you will be with me in paradise."

LUKE 23:43

TELL ME, WHAT HAS [THE THIEF ON THE CROSS] done to warrant help? He has wasted his life. Who is he to beg for forgiveness? He publicly scoffed at Jesus. What right does he have to pray, "Jesus, remember me when you come into your kingdom" (v. 42)?

Do you really want to know? The same right you have to pray.

You see, that is you and me on the cross. Naked, desolate, hopeless, and estranged. That is us. That is us asking.

We don't boast. We don't produce our list. Any sacrifice appears silly when placed before God on a cross.

We, like the thief, have one more prayer. And we, like the thief, pray.

And we, like the thief, hear the voice of grace.

He Still Moves Stones

April 29

Secondhand Spirituality

Come near to God, and God will come near to you.

James 4:8

Some of us have tried to have a daily quiet time and have not been successful. Others of us have a hard time concentrating. And all of us are busy. So rather than spend time with God, listening for his voice, we'll let others spend time with him and then benefit from their experience. Let them tell us what God is saying. After all, isn't that why we pay preachers?

If that is your approach, if your spiritual experiences are secondhand and not firsthand, I'd like to challenge you with this thought: Do you do that with other parts of your life?

You don't do that with vacations. . . . You don't do that with romance. . . . You don't let someone eat on your behalf, do you? [There are] certain things no one can do for you.

And one of those is spending time with God.

Just Like Jesus

April 30
Beggars in Need of Bread

"Give us the food we need for each day. Forgive us for our sins, just as we have forgiven those who sinned against us."

Matthew 6:11–12

We are sinners in need of grace, strugglers in need of strength. Jesus teaches us to pray, "Forgive us our debts . . . and lead us not into temptation (Matthew 6:12–13 niv)."

We've all made mistakes and we'll all make some more. The line that separates the best of us from the worst of us is a narrow one, hence we'd be wise to take seriously Paul's admonition: *Why do you judge your brothers or sisters in Christ? And why do you think you are better than they? We will all stand before God to be judged* (Romans 14:10).

Your sister would like me to remind you that she needs grace. Just like you need forgiveness, so does she. There comes a time in every relationship when it's damaging to seek justice, when settling the score only stirs the fire. There comes a time when the best thing you can do is accept your brother and offer him the same grace you've been given.

The Great House of God

MAY

Your word is like a lamp for my feet
and a light for my path.

—Psalm 119:105

May 1

Prayers Are Precious Jewels

The Lord sees the good people and listens to their prayers.

1 Peter 3:12

You and I live in a loud world. To get someone's attention is no easy task. He must be willing to set everything aside to listen: turn down the radio, turn away from the monitor, turn the corner of the page and set down the book. When someone is willing to silence everything else so he can hear us clearly, it is a privilege. A rare privilege, indeed.

[Your] prayers are honored [in heaven] as precious jewels. Purified and empowered, the words rise in a delightful fragrance to our Lord. . . . Your words do not stop until they reach the very throne of God.

Your prayer on earth activates God's power in heaven, and "God's will is done on earth as it is in heaven."

Your prayers move God to change the world. You may not understand the mystery of prayer. You don't need to. But this much is clear: Actions in heaven begin when someone prays on earth.

The Great House of God

May 2

We Look to God

"Lord, if it's you," Peter says, "tell me to come to you on the water."

Matthew 14:28 niv

Peter is not testing Jesus; he is pleading with Jesus. Stepping onto a stormy sea is not a move of logic; it is a move of desperation. Peter grabs the edge of the boat. Throws out a leg . . . follows with the other. Several steps are taken. It's as if an invisible ridge of rocks runs beneath his feet. At the end of the ridge is the glowing face of a never-say-die Friend.

We do the same, don't we? We come to Christ in an hour of deep need. We abandon the boat of good works. We realize . . . that human strength won't save us. So we look to God in desperation. We realize . . . that all the good works in the world are puny when laid before the Perfect One.

In the Eye of the Storm

May 3

Sometimes God Says No

Continue praying, keeping alert, and always thanking God.

Colossians 4:2

Can you imagine the outcome if a parent honored each request of each child during a trip? We'd inch our bloated bellies from one ice-cream store to the next.

Can you imagine the chaos if God indulged each of ours?

"For God has not *destined* us to the terrors of judgment, but to the full attainment of salvation through our Lord Jesus Christ" (1 Thessalonians 5:9 NEB, emphasis added).

Note God's destiny for your life. Salvation.

God's overarching desire is that you reach that destiny. His itinerary includes stops that encourage your journey. He frowns on stops that deter you. When his sovereign plan and your earthly plan collide, a decision must be made. Who's in charge of this journey?

If God must choose between your earthly satisfaction and your heavenly salvation, which do you hope he chooses?

Me too.

In the Eye of the Storm

May 4

God's Passion and Plan

Your word is like a lamp for my feet and a light for my path.

Psalm 119:105

The purpose of the Bible is simply to proclaim God's plan to save His children. It asserts that man is lost and needs to be saved. And it communicates the message that Jesus is the God in the flesh sent to save his children.

Though the Bible was written over sixteen centuries by at least forty authors, it has one central theme—salvation through faith in Christ. Begun by Moses in the lonely desert of Arabia and finished by John on the lonely Isle of Patmos, it is held together by a strong thread: God's passion and God's plan to save his children.

What a vital truth! Understanding the purpose of the Bible is like setting the compass in the right direction. Calibrate it correctly and you'll journey safely. But fail to set it, and who knows where you'll end up.

How to Study the Bible

May 5

Not Guilty

Who can accuse the people God has chosen? No one, because God is the One who makes them right.

Romans 8:33

Every moment of your life, your accuser is filing charges against you. He has noticed every error and marked each slip. Try to forget your past; he'll remind you. Try to undo your mistakes; he will thwart you.

This expert witness has no higher goal than to take you to court and press charges. Who is he? The devil.

He rails: "This one you call your child, God. He is not worthy."

As he speaks, you hang your head. You have no defense. His charges are fair. "I plead guilty, Your Honor," you mumble.

"The sentence?" Satan asks.

"The wages of sin is death," explains the Judge, "but in this case the death has already occurred. For this one died with Christ."

Satan is suddenly silent. And you are suddenly jubilant. . . . You have stood before the Judge and heard him declare, "Not guilty."

In the Grip of Grace

May 6

God's in Charge

God's Spirit, who is in you, is greater than the devil, who is in the world.

1 John 4:4

Satan has no power except that which God gives him.

To the first-century church in Smyrna, Christ said, "Do not be afraid of what you are about to suffer. I tell you, the devil will put some of you in prison to test you, and you will suffer for ten days. But be faithful, even if you have to die, and I will give you the crown of life" (Revelation 2:10).

Analyze Jesus' words for a minute. Christ informed the church of the persecution, the duration of the persecution (ten days), the reason for the persecution (to test you), and the outcome of the persecution (a crown of life). In other words, Jesus used Satan to fortify his church.

Even when [Satan] appears to win, he loses.

The Great House of God

May 7

Grace Teaches Us

He gave himself for us so he might pay the price to free us from all evil and to make us pure people who belong only to him.

Titus 2:14

Do we ever compromise tonight, knowing we'll confess tomorrow?

It's easy to be like the fellow visiting Las Vegas who called the preacher, wanting to know the hours of the Sunday service. The preacher was impressed. "Most people who come to Las Vegas don't do so to go to church."

"Oh, I'm not coming for the church. I'm coming for the gambling and parties and wild women. If I have half as much fun as I intend to, I'll need a church come Sunday morning."

Is that the intent of grace? Is God's goal to promote disobedience? Hardly. Grace "teaches us not to live against God nor to do the evil things the world wants us to do. Instead, that grace teaches us to live in the present age in a wise and right way and in a way that shows we serve God" (Titus 2:11–12). God's grace has released us from selfishness. Why return?

In the Grip of Grace

May 8

Get Out of the Judgment Seat

"You will be judged in the same way that you judge others."

Matthew 7:2

We condemn a man for stumbling this morning, but we didn't see the blows he took yesterday. We judge a woman for the limp in her walk, but we cannot see the tack in her shoe. We mock the fear in their eyes, but have no idea how many stones they have ducked or darts they have dodged.

Are they too loud? Perhaps they fear being neglected again. Are they too timid? Perhaps they fear failing again. Too slow? Perhaps they fell the last time they hurried. You don't know. Only one who has followed yesterday's steps can be their judge.

Not only are we ignorant about yesterday, we are ignorant about tomorrow. Dare we judge a book while chapters are yet unwritten? Should we pass a verdict on a painting while the artist still holds the brush? How can you dismiss a soul until God's work is complete? "God began doing a good work in you, and I am sure he will continue it until it is finished when Jesus Christ comes again" (Philippians 1:6).

In the Grip of Grace

May 9

LISTENING FOR GOD

A rule here, a rule there. A little lesson here, a little lesson there.

ISAIAH 28:10

EQUIPPED WITH THE RIGHT TOOLS, WE CAN LEARN to listen to God. What are those tools? Here are the ones I have found helpful.

A regular time and place. Select a slot on your schedule and a corner of your world, and claim it for God. For some it may be the best to do this in the morning. Others prefer the evening.

A second tool you need [is] an open Bible. God speaks to us through his Word. The first step in reading the Bible is to ask God to help you understand it. Don't go to Scripture looking for your own idea; go searching for God's.

There is a third tool. . . . Not only do we need a regular time and an open Bible, we also need a listening heart. If you want to be just like Jesus, let God have you. Spend time listening for him until you receive your lesson for the day—then apply it.

JUST LIKE JESUS

May 10

FAITH MEETS GRACE

Let us come near to God with a sincere heart and a sure faith, because we have been made free from a guilty conscience.

HEBREWS 10:22

FAITH IS NOT BORN AT THE NEGOTIATING TABLE where we barter our gifts in exchange for God's goodness. Faith is not an award given to the most learned. It's not a prize given to the most disciplined. It's not a title bequeathed to the most religious.

Faith is a desperate dive out of the sinking boat of human effort and a prayer that God will be there to pull us out of the water. The apostle Paul wrote about this kind of faith:

"For it is by grace you have been saved, through faith—and this not from yourselves, it is the gift of God—not by works, so that no one can boast" (Ephesians 2:8–9 NIV).

The supreme force in salvation is God's grace.

IN THE EYE OF THE STORM

May 11

Itemized Grace

The Lord knows those who belong to him.

2 Timothy 2:19

Imagine the event. You are before the judgment seat of Christ. The book is opened and the reading begins—each sin, each deceit, each occasion of destruction and greed. But as soon as the infraction is read, grace is proclaimed.

The result? God's merciful verdict will echo through the universe. For the first time in history, we will understand the depth of his goodness. Itemized grace. Catalogued kindness. Registered forgiveness. We will stand in awe as one sin after another is proclaimed, and then pardoned.

The devil will shrink back in defeat. The angels will step forward in awe. And we saints will stand tall in God's grace. As we see how much he has forgiven us, we will see how much he loves us. And we will worship him.

The result will be the first genuine community of forgiven people. Only one is worthy of the applause of heaven, and he's the one with the pierced hands and feet.

When Christ Comes

May 12

A Higher Standard

I keep trying to reach the goal and get the prize for which God called me.

Philippians 3:14

Most of my life I've been a closet slob. Then I got married.

I enrolled in a twelve-step program for slobs. ("My name is Max, I hate to vacuum.") A physical therapist helped me rediscover the muscles used for hanging shirts. My nose was reintroduced to the fragrance of Pine Sol.

Then came the moment of truth. Denalyn went out of town for a week. Initially I reverted to the old man. I figured I'd be a slob for six days and clean on the seventh. But something strange happened, a curious discomfort. I couldn't relax with dirty dishes in the sink.

What had happened to me? Simple. I'd been exposed to a higher standard.

Isn't that what has happened with us? Before Christ our lives were out of control, sloppy, and indulgent. We didn't even know we were slobs until we met him. Suddenly we find ourselves wanting to do good. Go back to the old mess? Are you kidding?

In the Grip of Grace

May 13

A Personal Query

Then Jesus asked, "But who do you say I am?"

Mark 8:29

Jesus turns [to his disciples] and asks them the question. *The* question. "But who do you say that I am?"

He doesn't ask, "What do you think about what I've done?" He asks, "Who do you say that I am?"

He doesn't ask, "Who do your friends think? Who do your parents think? Who do your peers think?" He poses instead a starkly personal query, "Who do you think I am?"

You have been asked some important questions in your life:

Will you marry me?

Would you be interested in a transfer?

What would you think if I told you I was pregnant?

You've been asked some important questions. But the grandest of them is an anthill compared to the Everest found in the eighth chapter of Mark.

"Who do you say I am?"

The Inspirational Study Bible

May 14

God's Mountains

"My grace is enough for you. When you are weak, my power is made perfect in you."

2 Corinthians 12:9

There are certain mountains only God can climb.

It's not that you aren't welcome to try, it's just that you aren't able.

If the word *Savior* is in your job description, it's because you put it there. Your role is to help the world, not save it. Mount Messiah is one mountain you weren't made to climb.

Nor is Mount Self-Sufficient. You aren't able to run the world, nor are you able to sustain it. Some of you think you can. You are self-made. You don't bow your knees, you just roll up your sleeves and put in another twelve-hour day . . . which may be enough when it comes to making a living or building a business. But when you face your own grave or your own guilt, your power will not do the trick.

The Great House of God

May 15

The Correct Solution

The just shall live by faith.

Romans 1:17 NKJV

At the moment I don't feel too smart. I just got off the wrong plane that took me to the wrong city and left me at the wrong airport. I went east instead of west and ended up in Houston instead of Denver.

It didn't look like the wrong plane, but it was. I walked through the wrong gate, dozed off on the wrong flight, and ended up in the wrong place.

Paul says we've all done the same thing. Not with airplanes and airports, but with our lives and God. He tells the Roman readers:

"There is none righteous, no, not one" (Romans 3:10 NKJV).

"All have sinned and fall short of the glory of God" (Romans 3:23).

We are all on the wrong plane, he said. All of us. Gentile and Jew. Every person has taken the wrong turn. And we need help. . . . The wrong solutions are pleasure and pride (Romans 1 and 2); the correct solution is Christ Jesus (Romans 3:21–26).

The Inspirational Study Bible

May 16

This Isn't Home

"I have chosen you out of the world, so you don't belong to it."

John 15:19

All of us know what it is like to be in a house that is not our own. Perhaps you've spent time in a dorm room or army barrack. Maybe you've slept in your share of hotels or bunked in a few hostels. They have beds. They have tables. They may have food and they may be warm, but they are a far cry from being "your father's house."

Your father's house is where your father is.

We don't always feel welcome here on earth. We wonder if there is a place here for us. People can make us feel unwanted. Tragedy leaves us feeling like intruders. Strangers. Interlopers in a land not ours. We don't always feel welcome here.

We shouldn't. This isn't our home. To feel unwelcome is no tragedy. Indeed it is healthy. We are not home here. This language we speak, it's not ours. This body we wear, it isn't us. And the world we live in, this isn't home.

A Gentle Thunder

May 17

No Nonsacred Moments

We are God's workers, working together.

1 Corinthians 3:9

It's a wonderful day indeed when we stop working for God and begin working with God.

For years I viewed God as a compassionate CEO and my role as a loyal sales representative. He had his office, and I had my territory. I could contact him as much as I wanted. He was always a phone or fax away. He encouraged me, rallied behind me, and supported me, but he didn't go with me. At least I didn't think he did. Then I read 2 Corinthians 6:1: We are "God's fellow workers" (niv).

Fellow workers? Co-laborers? God and I work together? Imagine the paradigm shift this truth creates. Rather than report to God, we work *with* God. Rather than check in with him and then leave, we check in with him and then follow. We are always in the presence of God. . . . There is never a nonsacred moment!

Just Like Jesus

May 18

Found, Called, and Adopted

"It is not the healthy people who need a doctor, but the sick. . . . I did not come to invite good people but to invite sinners."

Matthew 9:12–13

God didn't look at our frazzled lives and say, "I'll die for you when you deserve it."

No, despite our sin, in the face of our rebellion, he chose to adopt us. And for God, there's no going back. His grace is a come-as-you-are promise from a one-of-a-kind King. You've been found, called, and adopted; so trust your Father and claim this verse as your own: "God showed his love for us in this way: Christ died for us while we were still sinners" (Romans 5:8). And you never again have to wonder who your father is—you've been adopted by God and are therefore an "heir of God through Christ" (Galatians 4:7 NKJV).

In the Grip of Grace

May 19

Within Reach of Your Prayers

If God is for us, who can be against us?

Romans 8:31 niv

The question is not simply, "Who can be against us?" You could answer that one. Who is against you? Disease, inflation, corruption, exhaustion. Calamities confront, and fears imprison. Were Paul's question, "Who can be against us?" we could list our foes much easier than we could fight them. But that is not the question. The question is "If God is for us, *who can be against us?*" (emphasis added).

God is for you. Your parents may have forgotten you, your teachers may have neglected you, your siblings may be ashamed of you; but within reach of your prayers is the maker of the oceans. God!

In the Grip of Grace

May 20

God Is Angry at Evil

So put all evil things out of your life. . . .
These things make God angry.

—*Colossians 3:5–6*

Many don't understand God's anger because they confuse the wrath of God with the wrath of man. The two have little in common. Human anger is typically self-driven and prone to explosions of temper and violent deeds. We get ticked off because we've been overlooked, neglected, or cheated. This is the anger of man. It is not, however, the anger of God.

God doesn't get angry because he doesn't get his way. He gets angry because disobedience always results in self-destruction. What kind of father sits by and watches his child hurt himself?

In the Grip of Grace

May 21

God Knows You by Name

I have written your name on my hand.

Isaiah 49:16

Quite a thought, isn't it? Your name on God's hand. Your name on God's lips. Maybe you've seen your name in some special places. On an award or diploma. But to think that your name is on God's hand and on God's lips. . . . My, could it be?

Or perhaps you have never seen your name honored. And you can't remember when you heard it spoken with kindness. If so, it may be more difficult for you to believe that God knows your name.

But he does. Written on his hand. Spoken by his mouth. Whispered by his lips. Your name.

When God Whispers Your Name

May 22

The Brief Journey of Life

Our days on earth are like a shadow.

1 Chronicles 29:15 NIV

He who "lives forever" has placed himself at the head of a band of pilgrims who mutter, "How long, O Lord? . . . How long?" (Psalm 89:46 NIV).

"How long must I endure this sickness?"
"How long must I endure this spouse?"
"How long must I endure this paycheck?"

Do you really want God to answer? He could, you know. He could answer in terms of the here and now with time increments we know. "Two more years on the illness." "The rest of your life in the marriage." "Ten more years for the bills."

But he seldom does that. He usually opts to measure the here and now against the there and then. And when you compare this life to that life, this life ain't long.

In the Eye of the Storm

May 23

Keep Unity

May the Lord lead your hearts into God's love and Christ's patience.

2 Thessalonians 3:5

All people will know that you are my followers if you love each other" (John 13:35). Stop and think about this verse for a minute. Could it be that *unity* is the key to reaching the world for Christ?

If unity is the key to evangelism, shouldn't it have precedence in our prayers? Should we, as Paul said, "make every effort to keep the unity of the Spirit through the bond of peace" (Ephesians 4:3 NIV)? If unity matters to God, then shouldn't unity matter to us? If unity is a priority in heaven, then shouldn't it be a priority on earth?

Nowhere, by the way, are we told to build unity. We are told simply to keep unity. From God's perspective there is but "one flock and one shepherd" (John 10:16). Unity does not need to be created; it simply needs to be protected.

How do we do that? Does that mean we compromise our convictions? No. Does that mean we abandon the truths we cherish? No. But it does mean we look long and hard at the attitudes we carry.

In the Grip of Grace

May 24

Sorrow for Sin

If we confess our sins, he will forgive our sins,
because we can trust God to do what is right.

1 John 1:9

"If we confess our sins . . ." The biggest word in Scriptures just might be that two-letter one, *if.* For confessing sins—admitting failure—is exactly what prisoners of pride refuse to do.

"Me a sinner? Oh sure, I get rowdy every so often, but I'm a pretty good ol' boy."

"Listen, I'm just as good as the next guy. I pay my taxes."

Justification. Rationalization. Comparison. They sound good. They sound familiar. They even sound American. But in the kingdom, they sound hollow.

When you get to the point of sorrow for your sins, when you admit that you have no other option, then cast all your cares on him, for he is waiting.

The Applause of Heaven

May 25

Finding Courage in Grace

I was given mercy so that in me, the worst of all sinners, Christ Jesus could show that he has patience without limit.

1 Timothy 1:16

During the early days of the Civil War, a Union soldier was arrested on charges of desertion. Unable to prove his innocence, he was condemned and sentenced to die a deserter's death. His appeal found its way to the desk of Abraham Lincoln. The president felt mercy for the soldier and signed a pardon. The soldier returned to service, fought the entirety of the war, and was killed in the last battle. Found within his breast pocket was the signed letter of the president.

Close to the heart of the soldier were his leader's words of pardon. He found courage in grace. I wonder how many thousands more have found courage in the emblazoned cross of their heavenly King.

In the Grip of Grace

May 26

God Still Comes

The Lord is close to the brokenhearted, and he saves those whose spirits have been crushed.

Psalm 34:18

Everything that was written in the past was written to teach us," Paul pens. "The Scriptures give us patience and encouragement so that we can have hope" (Romans 15:4).

These are not just Sunday school stories. Not romantic fables. . . . They are historical moments in which a real God met real pain so we could answer the question, "Where is God when I hurt?"

How does God react to dashed hopes? Read the story of Jairus. How does the Father feel about those who are ill? Stand with him at the pool of Bethesda. Do you long for God to speak to your lonely heart? Then listen as he speaks to the Emmaus-bound disciples.

He's not doing it just for them. He's doing it for me. He's doing it for you.

The God who spoke still speaks. . . . The God who came still comes. He comes into our world. He comes into your world. He comes to do what you can't.

He Still Moves Stones

May 27

Intimacy with the Almighty

As a deer thirsts for streams of water, so I thirst for you, God.

Psalm 42:1

Jesus didn't act unless he saw his Father act. He didn't judge until he heard his Father judge. No act or deed occurred without his Father's guidance.

Because Jesus could hear what others couldn't, he acted differently than they did. Remember when everyone was troubled about the man born blind? Jesus wasn't. Somehow he knew that the blindness would reveal God's power (John 9:3). Remember when everyone was distraught about Lazarus's illness? Jesus wasn't. It was as if Jesus could hear what no one else could. Jesus had unbroken communion with his Father.

Do you suppose the Father desires the same for us? Absolutely! God desires the same abiding intimacy with you that he had with his Son.

Just Like Jesus

May 28

A Work in Progress

Jesus will keep you strong until the end so that there will be no wrong in you on the day our Lord Jesus Christ comes again.

1 Corinthians 1:8

God is not finished with you yet. Oh, you may think he is. You may think you've peaked. You may think he's got someone else to do the job.

If so, think again.

"God began doing a good work in you, and I am sure he will continue it until it is finished when Jesus Christ comes again" (Philippians 1:6).

Did you see what God is doing? "A good work in you."

Did you see when he will be finished? When Jesus comes again.

May I spell out the message? God ain't finished with you yet.

When God Whispers Your Name

May 29

Love Hates Evil

Many of those who sleep in the dust of the earth shall awake, some to everlasting life, and some to shame and everlasting contempt.

Daniel 12:2 RSV

Does hell serve a purpose? Remove it from the Bible and, at the same time, remove any notion of a just God and a trustworthy Scripture.

If there is no hell, God is not just. If there is no punishment of sin, heaven is apathetic toward the rapists and pillagers and mass murderers of society. If there is no hell, God is blind toward the victims and has turned his back on those who pray for relief. If there is no wrath toward evil, then God is not love, for love hates that which is evil.

To say there is no hell is also to say God is a liar and his Scripture untrue. The Bible repeatedly and stoutly affirms the dualistic outcome of history. Some will be saved. Some will be lost.

When Christ Comes

May 30

Beyond Our Faults

He felt sorry for them and healed those who were sick.

Matthew 14:14

Matthew writes that Jesus "healed their sick." Not *some* of their sick. Not the *righteous* among the sick. Not the *deserving* among the sick. But *the sick*.

Surely, among the many thousands, there were a few people unworthy of good health. The same divinity that gave Jesus the power to heal also gave him the power to perceive. I wonder if Jesus was tempted to say to the bigot, "Get out of here, buddy, and take your arrogance with you."

And he could see not only their past, but he could see their future.

Undoubtedly, there were those in the multitude who would use their newfound health to hurt others. Jesus released tongues that would someday curse. He gave sight to eyes that would lust. He healed hands that would kill.

Each time Jesus healed, he had to overlook the future and the past.

Something, by the way, that he still does.

In the Eye of the Storm

May 31

Play Sublimely

I praise you because you made me in an amazing and wonderful way.

Psalm 139:14

Antonio Stradivari was a seventeenth-century violin maker whose name in its Latin form, *Stradivarius*, has become synonymous with excellence. He once said that to make a violin less than his best would be to rob God, who could not make Antonio Stradivari's violins without Antonio.

He was right. God could not make Stradivarius violins without Antonio Stradivari. Certain gifts were given to that craftsman that no other violin maker possessed.

In the same vein, there are certain things you can do that no one else can. Perhaps it is parenting, or constructing houses, or encouraging the discouraged. There are things that only you can do, and you are alive to do them. In the great orchestra we call life, you have an instrument and a song, and you owe it to God to play them both sublimely.

The Applause of Heaven

JUNE

What we see will last only a short time,
but what we cannot see will last forever.

—2 Corinthians 4:18

June 1

God's Favorite Word

Jesus said, "Come follow me."

Matthew 4:19

God is an inviting God. He invited Mary to birth his Son, the disciples to fish for men, the adulteress woman to start over, and Thomas to touch his wounds. God is the King who prepares the palace, sets the table, and invites his subjects to come in.

In fact, it seems his favorite word is *come.*

"Come, let us talk about these things. Though your sins are like scarlet, they can be as white as snow" (Isaiah 1:18).

"All you who are thirsty, come and drink" (John 7:37).

"Come to me all, all of you who are tired and have heavy loads, and I will give you rest" (Matthew 11:28).

God is a God who invites. God is a God who calls.

And the Angels Were Silent

June 2

The Branch and the Vine

"Remain in me, and I will remain in you. A branch cannot produce fruit alone but must remain in the vine."

John 15:4

God wants to be as close to us as a branch is to a vine. One is an extension of the other. It's impossible to tell where one starts and the other ends. The branch isn't connected only at the moment of bearing fruit. The gardener doesn't keep the branches in a box and then, on the day he wants grapes, glue them to the vine. No, the branch constantly draws nutrition from the vine.

God also uses the temple to depict the intimacy he desires. "Don't you know," Paul writes, "that your body is the temple of the Holy Spirit, who lives in you and was given to you by God?" (1 Corinthians 6:19 TEV). Think with me about the temple for a moment. God didn't come and go, appear and disappear. He was a permanent presence, always available.

What incredibly good news for us! We are *never* away from God!

Just Like Jesus

June 3

A Hidden Hero

I have learned the secret of being happy at any time in everything that happens.

Philippians 4:12

Peer into the prison and see [Paul] for yourself: bent and frail, shackled to the arm of a Roman guard. Behold the apostle of God.

Dead broke. No family. No property. Nearsighted and worn out.

Doesn't look like a hero.

Doesn't sound like one either. He introduced himself as the worst sinner in history. He was a Christian-killer before he was a Christian leader. At times his heart was so heavy, Paul's pen drug itself across the page. "What a miserable man I am! Who will save me from this body that brings me death?" (Romans 7:24).

Only heaven knows how long he stared at the question before he found the courage to defy logic and write, "I thank God for saving me through Jesus Christ our Lord!" (Romans 7:25).

When God Whispers Your Name

June 4

POWER CAN BE PAINFUL

The wisdom of this world is foolishness with God.

1 CORINTHIANS 3:19

POWER COMES IN MANY FORMS.

It's the husband who refuses to be kind to his wife.

It's the employee who places personal ambition over personal integrity.

It's the wife who withholds sex both to punish and persuade.

It might be the taking of someone's life, or it might be the taking of someone's turn.

But they are all spelled the same: P-O-W-E-R. And all have the same goal: "I will get what I want at your expense."

And all have the same end: futility. Absolute power is unreachable. When you stand at the top—if there is a top—the only way to go is down. And the descent is often painful.

A thousand years from now, will it matter what title the world gave you? No, but it will make a literal hell of a difference whose child you are.

THE APPLAUSE OF HEAVEN

June 5

God's Mighty Hand

Through his power all things were made—things in heaven and on earth, things seen and unseen.

Colossians 1:16

With one decision, history began. Existence became measurable.

Out of nothing came light.

Out of light came day.

Then came sky . . . and earth.

And on this earth? A mighty hand went to work.

Canyons were carved. Oceans were dug. Mountains erupted out of flatlands. Stars were flung. A universe sparkled.

Look to the canyons to see the Creator's splendor. Touch the flowers and see his delicacy. Listen to the thunder and hear his power.

Today you will encounter God's creation. When you see the beauty around you, let each detail remind you to lift your head in praise. Express your appreciation for God's creation. Encourage others to see the beauty of his creation.

In the Eye of the Storm

June 6

The Oldest and Choicest

"Even when you are old, I will be the same. Even when your hair has turned gray, I will take care of you."

Isaiah 46:4

Growing old can be dangerous. The trail is treacherous and the pitfalls are many. One is wise to be prepared. You know it's coming. It's not like God kept the process a secret. It's not like you are blazing a trail as you grow older. It's not as if no one has ever done it before. Look around you. You have ample opportunity to prepare and ample case studies to consider. If growing old catches you by surprise, don't blame God. He gave you plenty of warning. He also gave you plenty of advice.

Your last chapters can be your best. Your final song can be your greatest. It could be that all of your life has prepared you for a grand exit. God's oldest have always been among his choicest.

He Still Moves Stones

June 7

God Will Get You Home

What we see will last only a short time, but what we cannot see will last forever.

2 Corinthians 4:18

For some of you, the journey has been long. Very long and stormy. In no way do I wish to minimize the difficulties that you have had to face along the way. Some of you have shouldered burdens that few of us could ever carry. You have bid farewell to lifelong partners. You have been robbed of life long dreams. You have been given bodies that can't sustain your spirit. You have spouses who can't tolerate your faith. You have bills that outnumber the paychecks and challenges that outweigh the strength.

And you are tired.

It's hard for you to see the City in the midst of the storms. The desire to pull over to the side of the road and get out entices you. You want to go on, but some days the road seems so long.

Let me encourage you. God never said that the journey would be easy, but he did say that the arrival would be worthwhile.

In the Eye of the Storm

June 8

Set Apart

Anyone who wants to be a friend of the world becomes God's enemy.

James 4:4

John the Baptist would never get hired today. No church would touch him. He was a public relations disaster. He "wore clothes made from camel's hair, had a leather belt around his waist, and ate locusts and wild honey" (Mark 1:6). Who would want to look at a guy like that every Sunday?

His message was as rough as his dress: a no-nonsense, bare-fisted challenge to repent because God was on his way.

John the Baptist set himself apart for one task, to be a voice of Christ. Everything about John centered on his purpose. His dress. His diet. His actions. His demands.

You don't have to be like the world to have an impact on the world. You don't have to be like the crowd to change the crowd. You don't have to lower yourself down to their level to lift them up to your level. Holiness doesn't seek to be odd. Holiness seeks to be like God.

A Gentle Thunder

June 9

God Honors Our Choice

We all have wandered away like sheep;
each of us has gone his own way.

Isaiah 53:6

How could a loving God send people to hell? That's a commonly asked question. The question itself reveals a couple of misconceptions.

First, God does not send people to hell. He simply honors their choice. Hell is the ultimate expression of God's high regard for the dignity of man. He has never forced us to choose him, even when that means we would choose hell.

No, God does not "send" people to hell. Nor does he send "people" to hell. That is the second misconception.

The word *people* is neutral, implying innocence. Nowhere does Scripture teach that innocent people are condemned. People do not go to hell. Sinners do. The rebellious do. The self-centered do. So how could a loving God send people to hell? He doesn't. He simply honors the choice of sinners.

When Christ Comes

June 10

Shortcuts

"They continue saying things that mean nothing, thinking that God will hear them because of their many words."

Matthew 6:7

I love short sentences. What follows are cuts from some of my books and a couple of others. Keep the ones you like. Forgive the ones you don't. Share them when you can.

Pray all the time. If necessary, use words.
God forgets the past. Imitate him.
Greed I've often regretted. Generosity—never.
Don't ask God to do what you want. Ask God to do what is right.
No one is useless to God. No one.
Nails didn't hold God to a cross. Love did.
You will never forgive anyone more than God has already forgiven you.

When God Whispers Your Name

June 11

Who's in Charge?

Give all your worries to him, because he cares about you.

1 Peter 5:7

Worry makes you forget who's in charge.

And when the focus is on yourself—you worry. You become anxious about many things. You worry that:

Your co-workers won't appreciate you.
Your leaders will overwork you.
Your superintendent won't understand you.
Your congregation won't support you.

With time, your agenda becomes more important than God's. You're more concerned with presenting self than pleasing him. And you may even find yourself doubting God's judgment.

God has gifted you with talents. He has done the same to your neighbor. If you concern yourself with your neighbor's talents, you will neglect yours. But if you concern yourself with yours, you could inspire both.

He Still Moves Stones

June 12

Walking with God

You were taught to be made new in your hearts, to become a new person. . . . made to be like God—made to be truly good and holy.

Ephesians 4:23–24

Healthy marriages have a sense of "remaining." The husband remains in the wife, and she remains in him. There is a tenderness, an honesty, an ongoing communication. The same is true in our relationship with God. Sometimes we go to him with our joys, and sometimes we go with our hurts, but we always go. And as we go, the more we go, the more we become like him. Paul says we are being changed from "glory to glory" (2 Corinthians 3:18 KJV).

People who live long lives together eventually begin to sound alike, to talk alike, even to think alike. As we walk with God, we take on his thoughts, his principles, his attitudes. We take on his heart.

Just Like Jesus

June 13

A Promise Delivered

I saw the holy city, the New Jerusalem, coming down out of heaven from God. It was prepared like a bride dressed for her husband.

Revelation 21:2

The Holy City, John says, is like "a bride beautifully dressed for her husband."

What is more beautiful than a bride?

Maybe it is the aura of whiteness that clings to her as dew clings to a rose. Or perhaps it is the diamonds that glisten in her eyes. Or maybe it's the blush of love that pinks her cheeks or the bouquet of promises she carries.

A bride. A commitment robed in elegance. "I'll be with you forever." Tomorrow bringing hope today. Promised purity faithfully delivered.

When you read that our heavenly home is similar to a bride, tell me, doesn't it make you want to go home?

The Applause of Heaven

June 14

The Cure for Disappointment

"I am the Lord, the God of every person on the earth. Nothing is impossible for me."

Jeremiah 32:27

We need to hear that God is still in control. We need to hear that it's not over until he says so. We need to hear that life's mishaps and tragedies are not a reason to bail out. They are simply a reason to sit tight.

Corrie ten Boom used to say, "When the train goes through a tunnel and the world gets dark, do you jump out? Of course not. You sit still and trust the engineer to get you through."

The way to deal with discouragement? The cure for disappointment? Go back and read the story of God. Read it again and again. Be reminded that you aren't the first person to weep. And you aren't the first person to be helped.

Read the story and remember, the story is yours!

He Still Moves Stones

June 15

The Big Choice

If you don't want to serve the Lord, you must choose for yourselves today whom you will serve.

Joshua 24:15

God's invitation is clear and nonnegotiable. He gives all and we give him all. Simple and absolute. He is clear in what he asks and clear in what he offers. The choice is up to us. Isn't it incredible that God leaves the choice to us? Think about it. There are many things in life we can't choose. We can't, for example, choose the weather. We can't control the economy.

We can't choose whether or not we are born with a big nose or blue eyes or a lot of hair. We can't even choose how people respond to us.

But we can choose where we spend eternity. The big choice, God leaves to us. The critical decision is ours.

That is the only decision that really matters.

And the Angels Were Silent

June 16

Needed: One Great Savior

All have sinned and are not good enough for God's glory, and all need to be made right with God by his grace, which is a free gift.

Romans 3:23–24

The supreme force in salvation is God's grace. Not our works. Not our talents. Not our feelings. Not our strength.

Salvation is God's sudden, calming presence during the stormy seas of our lives. We hear his voice; we take the step.

We, like Paul, are aware of two things: We are great sinners and we need a great savior.

We, like Peter, are aware of two facts: We are going down and God is standing up. So we leave behind the *Titanic* of self-righteousness and stand on the solid path of God's grace.

And, surprisingly, we are able to walk on water. Death is disarmed. Failures are forgivable. Life has real purpose. And God is not only within sight, he is within reach.

In the Eye of the Storm

June 17

Dealing with the Past

Don't get angry. Don't be upset; it only leads to trouble.

Psalm 37:8

Anger. It's easy to define: the noise of the soul. *Anger.* The unseen irritant of the heart. *Anger.* The relentless invader of silence.

The louder it gets, the more desperate we become.

Some of you are thinking, *You don't have any idea how hard my life has been.* And you're right. I don't. But I have a very clear idea how miserable your future will be unless you deal with your anger.

X-ray the world of the vengeful and behold the tumor of bitterness: black, menacing, malignant. Carcinoma of the spirit. Its fatal fibers creep around the edge of the heart and ravage it. Yesterday you can't alter, but your reaction to yesterday you can. The past you cannot change, but your response to your past you can.

When God Whispers Your Name

June 18

Who Is My Brother?

"Lord, how many times shall I forgive my brother when he sins against me?" Jesus answered, ". . . seventy-seven times."

Matthew 18:21–22 NIV

Seems to me God gives a lot more grace than we'd ever imagine.

We could do the same.

I'm not for watering down the truth or compromising the gospel. But if a fellow with a pure heart calls God "Father," can't I call that same man "Brother"? If God doesn't make doctrinal perfection a requirement for family membership, should I?

And if we never agree, can't we agree to disagree? If God can tolerate my mistakes, can't I tolerate the mistakes of others? If God allows me with my foibles and failures to call him "Father," shouldn't I extend the same grace to others?

When God Whispers Your Name

June 19

Living in God's Presence

Pray in the Spirit at all times with all kinds of prayers, asking for everything you need.

Ephesians 6:18

How do I live in God's presence? How do I detect his unseen hand on my shoulder and his inaudible voice in my ear? How can you and I grow familiar with the voice of God? Here are a few ideas:

Give God your waking thoughts. Before you face the day, face the Father. Before you step out of bed, step into his presence.

Give God your waiting thoughts. Spend time with him in silence.

Give God your whispering thoughts. Imagine considering every moment as a potential time of communion with God.

Give God your waning thoughts. At the end of the day, let your mind settle on him. Conclude the day as you began it: talking to God.

Just Like Jesus

June 20

A Heavenly Perspective

"Ask, and God will give to you. Search, and you will find. Knock, and the door will open for you."

Matthew 7:7

Go back and report to John what you hear and see: "The blind receive sight, the lame walk . . . and the good news is preached to the poor" (Luke 7:22 niv).

This was Jesus' answer to John's agonized query from the dungeon of doubt: "Are you the one who was to come, or should we expect someone else" (Luke 7:20)?

We don't know how John received Jesus' message, but we can imagine. I like to think of a slight smile coming over his lips as he heard what his Master said. For now he understood. It wasn't that Jesus was silent; it was that John had been listening for the wrong answer. John had been listening for an answer to his earthly problems, while Jesus was busy resolving his heavenly ones.

That's worth remembering the next time you hear the silence of God.

The Applause of Heaven

June 21

God Calls Your Name

This is what the Lord God says: I, myself, will search for my sheep and take care of them.

Ezekiel 34:11

He's waiting for you. God is standing on the porch of heaven, expectantly hoping, searching the horizon for a glimpse of his child. You're the one God is seeking.

God is the waiting Father, the caring Shepherd in search of his lamb. His legs are scratched, his feet are sore, and his eyes are burning. He scales the cliffs and traverses the fields. He explores the caves. He cups his hands to his mouth and calls into the canyon.

And the name he calls is yours.

The message is simple: God gave up his Son in order to rescue all his sons and daughters. To bring his children home. He's listening for your answer.

And the Angels Were Silent

June 22

A Little Light, Please

Jesus went to them, walking on the sea. . . .
And they cried out for fear.

Matthew 14:25–26 NKJV

Every so often a storm will come, and I'll look up into the blackening sky and say, "God, a little light, please?"

The light came for the disciples. A figure came to them walking on the water. It wasn't what they expected. Perhaps they were looking for angels to descend or heaven to open. . . . We don't know what they were looking for. But one thing is for sure, they weren't looking for Jesus to come walking on the water.

And since Jesus came in a way they didn't expect, they almost missed seeing the answer to their prayers.

And unless we look and listen closely, we risk making the same mistake. God's lights in our dark nights are as numerous as the stars, if only we'll look for them.

In the Eye of the Storm

June 23

PEACE TREATIES OF LOVE

Be sure that no one pays back wrong for wrong, but always try to do what is good for each other and for all people.

1 THESSALONIANS 5:15

JESUS DESCRIBED FOR HIS FOLLOWERS WHAT HE came to do. He came to build a relationship with people. He came to take away enmity, to take away the strife, to take away the isolation that existed between God and man. Once he bridged that—once he overcame that—he said, "I will call you friends."

In repairing a relationship, it's essential to realize that no friendship is perfect, no marriage is perfect, no person is perfect. With the resolve that you are going to make a relationship work, you can develop peace treaties of love and tolerance and harmony to transform a difficult situation into something beautiful.

WALKING WITH THE SAVIOR

June 24

A High-Stakes Mission

"Don't be afraid of people, who can kill the body but cannot kill the soul. The only one you should fear is the one who can destroy the soul and the body in hell."

Matthew 10:28

Hell's misery is deep, but not as deep as God's love.

So how do we apply this [truth]? If you are saved, it should cause you to rejoice. You've been rescued.

A glance into hell leads the believer to rejoice. But it also leads the believer to redouble his efforts to reach the lost. To understand hell is to pray more earnestly and to serve more diligently. Ours is a high-stakes mission.

And the lost? What is the meaning of this message for the unprepared? Heed the warnings and get ready. This plane won't fly forever. "Death is the destiny of every man; the living should take this to heart" (Ecclesiastes 7:2 niv).

When Christ Comes

June 25

What Is Your Price?

Life is not measured by how much one owns.

Luke 12:15

Jesus had a definition for *greed*. He called it "the practice of measuring life by possessions."

Greed equates a person's worth with a person's purse.

1. You got a lot = you are a lot.
2. You got a little = you are little.

The consequence of such a philosophy is predictable. If you are the sum of what you own, then by all means own it all. No price is too high. No payment is too much.

Greed is not defined by what something costs; it is measured by what it costs you.

If anything costs you your faith or your family, the price is too high.

When God Whispers Your Name

June 26

Secure in His Grasp

God is strong and can help you not to fall.

Jude v. 24

You and I are on a great climb. The wall is high, and the stakes are higher. You took your first step the day you confessed Christ as the Son of God. He gave you his harness—the Holy Spirit. In your hands he placed a rope—his Word.

Your first steps were confident and strong, but with the journey came weariness, and with the height came fear. You lost your footing. You lost your focus. You lost your grip, and you fell. For a moment, which seemed like forever, you tumbled wildly. Out of control. Out of self-control. Disoriented. Dislodged. Falling.

But then the rope tightened, and the tumble ceased. You hung in the harness and found it to be strong. You grasped the rope and found it to be true. And though you can't see your Guide, you know him. You know he is strong. You know he is able to keep you from falling.

A Gentle Thunder

June 27

Reflecting God's Glory

Our faces, then, are not covered. We all show the Lord's glory, and we are being changed to be like him.

2 Corinthians 3:18

The purpose of worship is to change the face of the worshiper. That is exactly what happened to Christ on the mountain. Jesus' appearance was changed: "His face became bright like the sun" (Matthew 17:2).

The connection between the face and worship is more than coincidental. Our face is the most public part of our bodies, covered less than any other area. It is also the most recognizable part of our bodies. We don't fill a yearbook with photos of people's feet but rather with photos of faces. God desires to take our faces, this exposed and memorable part of our bodies, and use them to reflect his goodness.

Just Like Jesus

June 28

Forgiveness Frees the Soul

If you suffer for doing good, and you are patient, then God is pleased.

1 Peter 2:20

Is there any emotion that imprisons the soul more than the unwillingness to forgive? What do you do when people mistreat you or those you love? Does the fire of anger boil within you, with leaping flames consuming your emotions? Or do you reach somewhere, to some source of cool water and pull out a bucket of mercy—to free yourself?

Don't get on the roller coaster of resentment and anger. You be the one who says, "Yes, he mistreated me, but I am going to be like Christ. I'll be the one who says, 'Forgive them, Father, they don't know what they're doing.'"

Walking with the Savior

June 29

A Soft Tap at the Door

But be holy in all you do, just as God,
the One who called you, is holy.

1 Peter 1:15

I have something against the lying voices that noise our world. You've heard them. They tell you to swap your integrity for a new sale. To barter your convictions for an easy deal. To exchange your devotion for a quick thrill.

They whisper. They woo. They taunt. They tantalize. They flirt. They flatter. "Go ahead, it's okay." "Don't worry. No one will know."

The world rams at your door; Jesus taps at your door. The voices scream for your allegiance; Jesus softly and tenderly requests it. The world promises flashy pleasure; Jesus promises a quiet dinner . . . with God.

Which voice do you hear?

In the Eye of the Storm

June 30

God, the Savior

"Those who believe in the Son have eternal life, but those who do not obey the Son will never have life."

John 3:36

When does salvation come?

When we look to Christ. When we embrace him as Savior. Astonishingly simple, isn't it? Claim the great promise of John 3:16: "God loved the world so much that he gave his one and only Son so that whoever believes in him may not be lost, but have eternal life."

God, the Lover. God, the Giver. God, the Savior.

And man, the believer. And for those who believe, God has promised a new birth.

But despite the simplicity, there are still those who don't believe. They don't trust the promise.

If only they would try. If only they would test it. But God is as polite as he is passionate. He never forces his way in. The choice is theirs.

A Gentle Thunder

JULY

Jesus spoke to them, saying, "Be of good cheer! It is I; do not be afraid."

—Matthew 14:27 NKJV

July 1

Judgment Is God's Job

Wait for the Lord, and he will make things right.

Proverbs 20:22

Some of you are in the courtroom. The courtroom of complaint. Some of you are rehashing the same hurt every chance you get with anyone who will listen.

For you, I have this question: Who made you God? I don't mean to be cocky, but why are you doing his work for him?

"Vengeance is Mine," God declared. "I will repay" (Hebrews 10:30 NKJV).

Judgment is God's job. To assume otherwise is to assume God can't do it.

Revenge is irreverent. To forgive someone is to display reverence. Forgiveness is not saying the one who hurt you was right. Forgiveness is stating that God is faithful and he will do what is right.

When God Whispers Your Name

July 2

Your Whispering Thoughts

God, examine me and know my heart; test me and know my anxious thoughts.

Psalm 139:23

Imagine considering every moment as a potential time of communion with God. By the time your life is over, you will have spent six months at stoplights, eight months opening junk mail, a year and a half looking for lost stuff (double that number in my case), and a whopping five years standing in various lines.

Why don't you give these moments to God? By giving God your whispering thoughts, the common becomes uncommon. Simple phrases such as "Thank you, Father," "Be sovereign in this hour, O Lord," and "You are my resting place, Jesus" can turn a commute into a pilgrimage. You needn't leave your office or kneel in your kitchen. Just pray where you are. Let the kitchen become a cathedral or the classroom a chapel. Give God your whispering thoughts.

Just Like Jesus

July 3

God Changes Our Face

He put a new song in my mouth, a song of praise to our God.

Psalm 40:3

God invites us to see his face so he can change ours. He uses our uncovered faces to display his glory. The transformation isn't easy. The sculptor of Mount Rushmore faced a lesser challenge than God does. But our Lord is up to the task. He loves to change the faces of his children. By his fingers, wrinkles of worry are rubbed away. Shadows of shame and doubt become portraits of grace and trust. He relaxes clenched jaws and smooths furrowed brows. His touch can remove the bags of exhaustion from beneath the eyes and turn tears of despair into tears of peace.

How? Through worship.

We'd expect something more complicated, more demanding. A forty-day fast or the memorization of Leviticus perhaps. No. God's plan is simpler. He changes our faces through worship.

Just Like Jesus

July 4

Finding God's Grace

You gave me life and showed me kindness, and in your care you watched over my life.

Job 10:12

Discipline is easy for me to swallow. Logical to assimilate. Manageable and appropriate. But God's grace? Anything but. Examples? How much time do you have?

David the psalmist becomes David the voyeur, but by God's grace becomes David the psalmist again.

Peter denied Christ before he preached Christ.

Zacchaeus, the crook: the cleanest part of his life was the money he'd laundered. But Jesus still had time for him.

The thief on the cross: hell-bent and hung-out-to-die one minute, heaven-bound and smiling the next.

Story after story. Prayer after prayer. Surprise after surprise. Seems that God is looking more for ways to get us home than ways to keep us out. I challenge you to find one soul who came to God seeking grace and did not find it.

When God Whispers Your Name

July 5

The Dungeon of Bitterness

"If you forgive others for their sins, your Father in heaven will also forgive you for your sins."

Matthew 6:14

Bitterness is its own prison.

The sides are slippery with resentment. A floor of muddy anger stills the feet. The stench of betrayal fills the air and stings the eyes. A cloud of self-pity blocks the view of the tiny exit above.

Step in and look at the prisoners. Victims are chained to the walls. Victims of betrayal. Victims of abuse.

The dungeon, deep and dark, is beckoning you to enter. You can, you know. You've experienced enough hurt. You can choose, like many, to chain yourself to your hurt. Or you can choose, like some, to put away your hurts before they become hates.

How does God deal with your bitter heart? He reminds you that what you have is more important than what you don't have. You still have your relationship with God. No one can take that.

He Still Moves Stones

July 6
THE PERFECT PRIEST

On the day when the Lord Jesus comes . . . all the people who have believed will be amazed at Jesus.

2 THESSALONIANS 1:10

WHEN WE SEE CHRIST, WHAT WILL WE SEE?

We will see the perfect priest. "He was dressed in a long robe and had a gold band around his chest" (Revelation 1:13). The first readers of this message knew the significance of the robe and band. Jesus is wearing the clothing of a priest. A priest presents people to God and God to people.

You have known other priests. There have been others in your life, whether clergy or not, who sought to bring you to God. But they, too, needed a priest. Some needed a priest more than you did. They, like you, were sinful. Not so with Jesus. "Jesus is the kind of high priest we need. He is holy, sinless, pure, not influenced by sinners, and he is raised above the heavens" (Hebrews 7:26).

Jesus is the perfect priest.

WHEN CHRIST COMES

July 7

Closer Than You Think

Jesus spoke to them, saying, "Be of good cheer! It is I; do not be afraid."

Matthew 14:27 NKJV

When the disciples saw Jesus in the middle of their stormy night, they called him a ghost. A phantom. To them, the glow was anything but God.

When we see gentle lights on the horizon, we often have the same reaction. We dismiss occasional kindness as apparitions, accidents, or anomalies. Anything but God.

And because we look for the bonfire, we miss the candle. Because we listen for the shout, we miss the whisper.

But it is in burnished candles that God comes, and through whispered promises he speaks: "When you doubt, look around; I am closer than you think."

In the Eye of the Storm

July 8

He Kept the Faith

Continue to have faith and do what you know is right. Some people have rejected this, and their faith has been shipwrecked.

1 Timothy 1:19

I sit a few feet from a man on death row. Jewish by birth. Tentmaker by trade. Apostle by calling. His days are marked. I'm curious about what bolsters this man as he nears his execution. So I ask some questions.

Do you have family, Paul? *I have none.*

What about your health? *My body is beaten and tired.*

Any awards? *Not on earth.*

Then what do you have, Paul? No belongings. No family. What do you have that matters?

I have my faith. It's all I have. But it's all I need. I have kept the faith.

Paul leans back against the wall of his cell and smiles.

When God Whispers Your Name

July 9

A Father's Pride

God is being patient with you. He does not want anyone to be lost, but he wants all people to change their hearts and lives.

2 Peter 3:9

To those who embrace Christ as Savior, he has promised a new birth.

Does that mean the old nature will never rear its ugly head? Does that mean you will instantly be able to resist any temptation?

To answer that question, compare your new birth in Christ to a newborn baby. Can a newborn walk? Can he feed himself? Can he sing or read or speak? No, not yet. But someday he will.

It takes time to grow. But is the parent in the delivery room ashamed of the baby? Is the mom embarrassed that the infant can't spell . . . that the baby can't walk . . . that the newborn can't give a speech?

Of course not. The parents aren't ashamed; they are proud. They know that growth will come with time. So does God.

A Gentle Thunder

July 10

The Purpose of Life

"Love the Lord your God with all your heart, all your soul, and all your mind."

Matthew 22:37

Mine deep enough in every heart and you'll find it: a longing for meaning, a quest for purpose. As surely as a child breathes, he will someday wonder, "What is the purpose of my life?"

Some search for meaning in a career. "My purpose is to be a dentist." Fine vocation but hardly a justification for existence.

For others, who they are is what they have. They find meaning in a new car or a new house or new clothes. These people are great for the economy and rough on the budget because they are always seeking meaning in something they own. Some try sports, entertainment, cults, sex, you name it.

All mirages in the desert of purpose.

Shouldn't we face the truth? If we don't acknowledge God, we are flotsam in the universe.

In the Grip of Grace

July 11

A Big View of God

Holy, holy, holy is the Lord God Almighty.
He was, he is, and he is coming.

Revelation 4:8

Exactly what is worship? I like King David's definition. "O magnify the Lord with me, and let us exalt His name together" (Psalm 34:3 NASB). Worship is the act of magnifying God. Enlarging our vision of him. Stepping into the cockpit to see where he sits and observe how he works. Of course, his size doesn't change, but our perception of him does. As we draw nearer, he seems larger. Isn't that what we need? A *big* view of God? Don't we have *big* problems, *big* worries, *big* questions? Of course we do. Hence we need a big view of God.

Worship offers that. How can we sing "Holy, holy, holy" and not have our vision expanded?

Just Like Jesus

July 12

Repentance Is a Decision

Perhaps you do not understand that God is kind to you so you will change your hearts and lives.

Romans 2:4

No one is happier than the one who has sincerely repented of wrong. Repentance is the decision to turn from selfish desires and seek God. It is a genuine, sincere regret that creates sorrow and moves us to admit wrong and desire to do better.

It's an inward conviction that expresses itself in outward actions.

You look at the love of God and you can't believe he's loved you like he has, and this realization motivates you to change your life. That is the nature of repentance.

Walking with the Savior

July 13

Knowing God's Will

"Those who see the Son and believe in him have eternal life. . . . This is what my Father wants."

John 6:40

We learn God's will by spending time in his presence. The key to knowing God's heart is having a relationship with him. A *personal* relationship. God will speak to you differently than he will speak to others. Just because God spoke to Moses through a burning bush, that doesn't mean we should all sit next to a bush waiting for God to speak. God used a fish to convict Jonah. Does that mean we should have worship services at Sea World? No. God reveals his heart personally to each person.

For that reason, your walk with God is essential. His heart is not seen in an occasional chat or weekly visit. We learn his will as we take up residence in his house every single day.

Walk with him long enough and you come to know his heart.

The Great House of God

July 14

God's Signature

Before I made you in your mother's womb, I chose you.

Jeremiah 1:5

With God in your world, you aren't an accident or an incident; you are a gift to the world, a divine work of art, signed by God.

One of the finest gifts I ever received is a football signed by thirty former professional quarterbacks. There is nothing unique about this ball. For all I know it was bought at a discount sports store. What makes it unique are the signatures.

The same is true with us. In the scheme of nature, Homo sapiens are not unique. We aren't the only creatures with flesh and hair and blood and hearts. What makes us special is not only our body, but also the signature of God on our lives. We are his works of art. We are created in his image to do good deeds. We are significant, not because of what we do, but because of whose we are.

In the Grip of Grace

July 15

More Than Meets the Eye

Faith means being sure of the things we hope for and knowing that something is real even if we do not see it.

Hebrews 11:1

Faith is trusting what the eye can't see.

Eyes see the prowling lion. Faith sees Daniel's angel.
Eyes see storms. Faith sees Noah's rainbow.
Eyes see giants. Faith sees Canaan.
Your eyes see your faults. Your faith sees your Savior.
Your eyes see your guilt. Your faith sees his blood.

Your eyes look in the mirror and see a sinner, a failure, a promise-breaker. But by faith you look in the mirror and see a robed prodigal bearing the ring of grace on your finger and the kiss of your Father on your face.

When God Whispers Your Name

July 16

All God's Children

If they could be made God's people by what they did,
God's gift of grace would not really be a gift.

Romans 11:6

To whom does God offer his gift? To the brightest? The most beautiful or the most charming? No. His gift is for us all—bankers and beggars, clergy and clerks, judges and janitors. All God's children.

And he wants us so badly, he'll take us in any condition; "as is" reads the tag on our collars. He's not about to wait for us to reach perfection (he knows we'll never get there!). Do you think he's waiting for us to overcome all temptations? Hardly. When we master the Christian walk? Far from it. Remember, Christ died for us when we were still sinners. His sacrifice, then, was not dependent on our performance.

He wants us now.

No Wonder They Call Him the Savior

July 17

God Is in Your Corner

He will not leave you or forget you.

Deuteronomy 31:8

When I was seven years old, I ran away from home. I'd had enough of my father's rules and decided I could make it on my own, thank you very much. With my clothes in a paper bag, I stormed out the back gate and marched down the alley. [But] I didn't go far. I got to the end of the alley and remembered I was hungry, so I went back home.

Though the rebellion was brief, it was rebellion nonetheless. And had you stopped me on that prodigal path . . . I just might have told you how I felt. I just might have said, "I don't need a father. I'm too big for the rules of my family."

I didn't hear the rooster crow like Peter did. I didn't feel the fish belch like Jonah did. I didn't get a robe and a ring and sandals like the prodigal did. But I learned from my father on earth what those three learned from their Father in heaven. Our God is no fair-weather Father. He's not into this love-'em-and-leave-'em stuff. I can count on him to be in my corner no matter how I perform. You can too.

The Great House of God

July 18

God Walks Among the Suffering

He took our suffering on him and carried our diseases.

Matthew 8:17

Picture a battleground strewn with wounded bodies, and you see Bethesda. Imagine a nursing home overcrowded and understaffed, and you see the pool. Call to mind the orphans in Bangladesh or the abandoned in New Delhi, and you will see what people saw when they passed Bethesda. As they passed, what did they hear? An endless wave of groans. What did they witness? A field of faceless need. What did they do? Most walked past.

But not Jesus.

He is alone. The people need him—so he's there. Can you picture it? Jesus walking among the suffering.

Little do they know that God is walking slowly, stepping carefully between the beggars and the blind.

He Still Moves Stones

July 19

Why Deny?

If we say we have no sin, we are fooling ourselves, and the truth is not in us.

1 John 1:8

We do ourselves no favors in justifying our deeds or glossing over our sins. Some time ago my daughter Andrea got a splinter in her finger. I took her to the restroom and set out some tweezers, ointment, and a Band-Aid.

She didn't like what she saw. "I just want the Band-Aid, Daddy."

Sometimes we are just like Andrea. We come to Christ with our sin, but all we want is a covering. We want to skip the treatment. We want to hide our sin. And one wonders if God, even in his great mercy, will heal what we conceal.

How can God heal what we deny? How can God touch what we cover up?

A Gentle Thunder

July 20

We Shall See Him

Now we see a dim reflection, as if we were looking into a mirror, but then we shall see clearly.

1 Corinthians 13:12

What will happen when you see Jesus?

You will see unblemished purity and unbending strength. You will feel his unending presence and know his unbridled protection. And—all that he is, you will be, for you will be like Jesus. Wasn't that the promise of John? "We know that when Christ comes again, we will be like him, because we will see him as he really is" (1 John 3:2).

Since you'll be pure as snow, you will never sin again; you will never stumble again; you will never feel lonely again; you will never doubt again.

When Christ comes, you will dwell in the light of God. And you will see him as he really is.

When Christ Comes

July 21

Getting Our Attention

Come back to the Lord your God, because he is kind and shows mercy. He doesn't become angry quickly, and he has great love.

Joel 2:13

How far do you want God to go in getting your attention? If God has to choose between your eternal safety and your earthly comfort, which do you hope he chooses?

What if he moved you to another land? (As he did Abraham.) What if he called you out of retirement? (Remember Moses?) How about the voice of an angel or the bowel of a fish? (A la Gideon and Jonah.) How about a promotion like Daniel's or a demotion like Samson's?

God does what it takes to get our attention. Isn't that the message of the Bible? The relentless pursuit of God. God on the hunt. God in the search. Peeking under the bed for hiding kids, stirring the bushes for lost sheep.

A Gentle Thunder

July 22

If Only . . .

"Spiritual life comes from the Spirit."

John 3:6

Maybe your past isn't much to brag about. Maybe you've seen raw evil. And now you have to make a choice. Do you rise above the past and make a difference? Or do you remain controlled by the past and make excuses?

Many choose the convalescent homes of the heart. Healthy bodies. Sharp minds. But retired dreams. Back and forth they rock in the chair of regret, repeating the terms of surrender. Lean closely and you will hear them:

"If only."

"If only I'd been born somewhere else."

"If only I'd been treated fairly."

Maybe you've used those words. Maybe you have every right to use them. If such is the case . . . go to John's gospel and read Jesus' words: "Human life comes from human parents, but spiritual life comes from the Spirit" (John 3:6).

When God Whispers Your Name

July 23

Heed the Signals

Honor God and obey his commands,
because this is all people must do.

Ecclesiastes 12:13

Here are some God-given, time-tested truths that define the way you should navigate your life. Observe them and enjoy secure passage. Ignore them and crash against the ragged rocks of reality:

- Love God more than you fear hell.
- Make major decisions in a cemetery.
- When no one is watching, live as if someone is.
- Succeed at home first.
- Don't spend tomorrow's money today.
- Pray twice as much as you fret.
- God has forgiven you; you'd be wise to do the same.

In the Eye of the Storm

July 24

Lifting Heart and Hands

To the King that rules forever, who will never die, who cannot be seen, the only God, be honor and glory forever and ever.

1 Timothy 1:17

The whole purpose of coming before the King is to praise him, to live in recognition of his splendor. Praise—lifting up our heart and hands, exulting with our voices, singing his praises—is the occupation of those who dwell in the kingdom.

Praise is the highest occupation of any being. What happens when we praise the Father? We reestablish the proper chain of command; we recognize that the King is on the throne and that he has saved his people.

Walking with the Savior

July 25

What Size Is God?

"God can do all things."

Matthew 19:26

Nature is God's workshop. The sky is his resume. The universe is his calling card. You want to know who God is? See what he has done. You want to know his power? Take a look at his creation. Curious about his strength? Pay a visit to his home address: 1 Billion Starry Sky Avenue.

He is untainted by the atmosphere of sin, unbridled by the timeline of history, unhindered by the weariness of the body.

What controls you doesn't control him. What troubles you doesn't trouble him. What fatigues you doesn't fatigue him. Is an eagle disturbed by traffic? No, he rises above it. Is the whale perturbed by a hurricane? Of course not—he plunges beneath it. Is the lion flustered by the mouse standing directly in his way? No, he steps over it.

How much more is God able to soar above, plunge beneath, and step over the troubles of the earth!

The Great House of God

July 26

The Answer to Arguments

Get along with each other, and forgive each other. If someone does wrong to you, forgive that person because the Lord forgave you.

COLOSSIANS 3:13

UNITY DOESN'T BEGIN IN EXAMINING OTHERS BUT IN examining self. Unity begins not in demanding that others change, but in admitting that we aren't so perfect ourselves.

The answer to arguments? Acceptance. The first step to unity? Acceptance. Not agreement, acceptance. Not unanimity; acceptance. Not negotiation, arbitration, or elaboration. Those might come later, but only after the first step: acceptance.

IN THE GRIP OF GRACE

July 27

Christ's Ultimate Aim

"He came to serve others and to give his life as a ransom for many people."

Mark 10:45

One of the incredible abilities of Jesus was to stay on target. His life never got off track. . . . He kept his life on course.

As Jesus looked across the horizon of his future, he could see many targets. Many flags were flapping in the wind, each of which he could have pursued. He could have been a political revolutionary. He could have been content to be a teacher and educate minds. But in the end he chose to be a Savior and save souls.

Anyone near Christ for any length of time heard it from Jesus himself. "The Son of Man came to find lost people and save them" (Luke 19:10). The heart of Christ was relentlessly focused on one task. The day he left the carpentry shop of Nazareth he had one ultimate aim—the cross of Calvary.

Just Like Jesus

July 28

Don't Be Troubled

The person who trusts the Lord will be blessed.

Jeremiah 17:7

Just prior to his crucifixion, [Jesus] told his disciples that he would be leaving them. "Where I am going you cannot follow now, but you will follow later" (John 13:36).

Such a statement was bound to stir some questions. Peter spoke for the others and asked, "Lord, why can't I follow you now?" (v. 37).

See if Jesus' reply doesn't reflect the tenderness of a parent to a child: "Don't let your hearts be troubled. Trust in God, and trust in me. There are many rooms in my Father's house; I would not tell you this it if were not true. I am going there to prepare a place for you. . . . I will come back and take you to be with me so that you may be where I am" (John 14:1–3).

Reduce the paragraph to a sentence and it might read: "You do the trusting and I'll do the taking."

When Christ Comes

July 29

No Fears at All

I am the Lord your God, who holds your right hand, and I tell you, "Don't be afraid. I will help you."

Isaiah 41:13

Could you use some courage? Are you backing down more than you are standing up? Jesus scattered the butterflies out of the stomachs of his nervous disciples.

We need to remember that the disciples were common men given a compelling task. Before they were the stained-glassed saints in the windows of cathedrals, they were somebody's next-door neighbors trying to make a living and raise a family. They weren't cut from theological cloth or raised on supernatural milk. But they were an ounce more devoted than they were afraid and, as a result, did some extraordinary things.

Earthly fears are no fears at all. Answer the big question of eternity, and the little questions of life fall into perspective.

The Applause of Heaven

July 30

God Gives Rest

"The burden that I ask you to accept is easy;
the load I give you to carry is light."

Matthew 11:30

Paul had an interesting observation about the way we treat people. He said it about marriage, but the principle applies in any relationship. "The man who loves his wife loves himself" (Ephesians 5:28). There is a correlation between the way you feel about yourself and the way you feel about others. If you are at peace with yourself—if you like yourself—you will get along with others.

The converse is also true. If you don't like yourself, if you are ashamed, embarrassed, or angry, other people are going to know it.

Which takes us to the question "How does a person get relief?"

"Come to me, all of you who are tired and have heavy loads, and I will give you rest" (Matthew 11:28). Jesus says he is the solution for weariness of soul.

When God Whispers Your Name

July 31

He's Coming Back

Christ rose first; then when Christ comes back, all his people will become alive again.

1 Corinthians 15:23 TLB

God has made [a] promise to us. "I will come back," he assures us. Yes, the rocks will tumble. Yes, the ground will shake. But the child of God needn't fear, for the Father has promised to take us to be with him.

But dare we believe the promise? Dare we trust his loyalty? Isn't there a cautious part of us that wonders how reliable these words may be?

How can we know he will do what he said? How can we believe he will move the rocks and set us free?

Because he's already done it once.

When Christ Comes

AUGUST

But grow in the grace and knowledge of our Lord and Savior Jesus Christ.

—2 PETER 3:18 NIV

August 1

Nothing on Earth Satisfies

We brought nothing into the world, so we can take nothing out. But, if we have food and clothes, we will be satisfied with that.

1 Timothy 6:7–8

Satisfied? That is one thing we are not. We are not satisfied.

We take a vacation of a lifetime. We satiate ourselves with sun, fun, and good food. But we are not even on the way home before we dread the end of the trip and begin planning another.

We are not satisfied.

As a child we say, "If only I were a teenager." As a teen we say, "If only I were an adult." As an adult, "If only I were married." As a spouse, "If only I had kids."

We are not satisfied. Contentment is a difficult virtue. Why?

Because there is nothing on earth that can satisfy our deepest longing. We long to see God. The leaves of life are rustling with the rumor that we will—and we won't be satisfied until we do.

When God Whispers Your Name

August 2

The Master Builder

He restores my soul; He leads me in the paths of righteousness for His name's sake.

Psalm 23:3 NKJV

It's hard to see things grow old. The town in which I grew up is growing old. Some of the buildings are boarded up. Some of the houses are torn down. The old movie house where I took my dates has For Sale on the marquee.

I wish I could make it all new again. I wish I could blow the dust off the streets . . . but I can't.

I can't. But God can. "He restores my soul," wrote the shepherd. God doesn't reform; he restores. He doesn't camouflage the old; he restores the new. The Master Builder will pull out the original plan and restore it. He will restore the vigor. He will restore the energy. He will restore the hope. He will restore the soul.

The Applause of Heaven

August 3

A Raging Fire

Since God has shown us great mercy, I beg you to offer your lives as a living sacrifice to him.

Romans 12:1

Resentment is the cocaine of the emotions. It causes our blood to pump and our energy level to rise. But, also like cocaine, it demands increasingly large and more frequent dosages. There is a dangerous point at which anger ceases to be an emotion and becomes a driving force. A person bent on revenge moves unknowingly further and further away from being able to forgive, for to be without the anger is to be without a source of energy.

Hatred is the rabid dog that turns on its owner.

Revenge is the raging fire that consumes the arsonist.

Bitterness is the trap that snares the hunter.

And mercy is the choice that can set them all free.

The Applause of Heaven

August 4

You Have Captured God's Heart

As a man rejoices over his new wife, so
your God will rejoice over you.

Isaiah 62:5

Have you ever noticed the way a groom looks at his bride during the wedding? I have. Perhaps it's my vantage point. As the minister of the wedding, I'm positioned next to the groom.

If the light is just so and the angle just right, I can see a tiny reflection in his eyes. Her reflection. And the sight of her reminds him why he is here. His jaw relaxes and his forced smile softens. He forgets he's wearing a tux. He forgets his sweat-soaked shirt. When he sees her, any thought of escape becomes a joke again. For it's written all over his face, "Who could bear to live without this bride?"

And such are precisely the feelings of Jesus. Look long enough into the eyes of our Savior and, there, too, you will see a bride. Dressed in fine linen. Clothed in pure grace . . . she is the bride . . . walking toward him.

And who is this bride for whom Jesus longs? You are. You have captured the heart of God.

When Christ Comes

August 5

God's Plans

Enjoy serving the Lord, and he will give you what you want.

Psalm 37:4

When we submit to God's plans, we can trust our desires. Our assignment is found at the intersection of God's plan and our pleasures. *What do you love to do? What brings you joy? What gives you a sense of satisfaction?*

Some long to feed the poor. Others enjoy leading the church. . . . Each of us has been made to serve God in a unique way.

The longings of your heart, then, are not incidental; they are critical messages. The desires of your heart are not to be ignored; they are to be consulted. As the wind turns the weather vane, so God uses your passions to turn your life. God is too gracious to ask you to do something you hate.

Just Like Jesus

August 6

Our Problem Is Sin

Fix your attention on God. You'll be changed from the inside out.

Romans 12:2 msg

Real change is an inside job. You might alter things a day or two with money and systems, but the heart of the matter is, and always will be, the matter of the heart.

Allow me to get specific. Our problem is sin. Not finances. Not budgets. . . . Sin. We are in rebellion against our Creator. We are separated from our Father. We are cut off from the source of life. A new president or policy won't fix that. It can only be solved by God.

That's why the Bible uses drastic terms like *conversion, repentance,* and *lost and found.* Society may renovate, but only God recreates.

When God Whispers Your Name

August 7

Truth in Love

Your kingdom is built on what is right and fair. Love and truth are in all you do.

Psalm 89:14

The single most difficult pursuit is truth and love.

That sentence is grammatically correct. I know every English teacher would like to pluralize it to read: The most difficult pursuits are those of truth and love. But that's not what I mean to say.

Love is a difficult pursuit.
Truth is a tough one too.

But put them together, pursue truth and love at the same time, and hang on, baby, you're in for the ride of your life.

Love in truth. Truth in love. Never one at the expense of the other. Never the embrace of love without the torch of truth. Never the heat of truth without the warmth of love.

To pursue both is our singular task.

The Inspirational Study Bible

August 8

Safe to Believe

When Jesus was raised from the dead it was a signal of the end of death-as-the-end.

Romans 6:6 msg

Don't you love that sentence? "It was the signal of the end of death-as-the-end." The resurrection is an exploding flare announcing to all sincere seekers that it is safe to believe. Safe to believe in ultimate justice. Safe to believe in eternal bodies. Safe to believe in heaven as our estate and the earth as its porch. Safe to believe in a time when questions won't keep us awake and pain won't keep us down. Safe to believe in open graves and endless days and genuine praise.

Because we can accept the resurrection story, it is safe to accept the rest of the story.

When Christ Comes

August 9

The True Son of God

His followers went to him and woke him, saying, "Lord, save us! We will drown!" Jesus answered, "Why are you afraid?"

Matthew 8:25–26

Read this verse: "Then those who were in the boat worshiped him, saying, 'Truly you are the Son of God'" (Matthew 14:33 niv).

After the storm, [the disciples] worshiped him. They had never, as a group, done that before. Never. Check it out. Open your Bible. Search for a time when the disciples corporately praised him.

You won't find it.

You won't find them worshiping when he healed the leper. Forgave the adulteress. Preached to the masses. They were willing to follow. Willing to leave family. Willing to cast out demons. Willing to be in the army.

But only after the incident on the sea did they worship him. Why?

Simple. This time they were the ones who were saved.

In the Eye of the Storm

August 10

A Parent's Precious Prayers

All your children will be taught by the Lord,
and they will have much peace.

Isaiah 54:13

Never underestimate the ponderings of a Christian parent. Never underestimate the power that comes when a parent pleads with God on behalf of a child. Who knows how many prayers are being answered right now because of the faithful ponderings of a parent ten or twenty years ago? God listens to thoughtful parents.

Praying for our children is a noble task. If what we are doing in this fast-paced society is taking us away from prayer time for our children, we're doing too much. There is nothing more special, more precious than time that a parent spends struggling and pondering with God on behalf of a child.

Walking with the Savior

August 11

To See the Unseen

He gives strength to those who are tired and
more power to those who are weak.

Isaiah 40:29

An example of faith was found on the wall of a concentration camp. On it a prisoner had carved the words:

> I believe in the sun, even though it doesn't shine,
> I believe in love, even when it isn't shown,
> I believe in God, even when he doesn't speak.

I try to imagine the person who etched those words. I try to envision his skeletal hand gripping the broken glass or stone that cut into the wall. I try to imagine his eyes squinting through the darkness as he carved each letter. What hand could have cut such a conviction? What eyes could have seen good in such horror?

There is only one answer: eyes that chose to see the unseen.

He Still Moves Stones

August 12

Infinite Patience

Patience produces character, and character produces hope. And this hope will never disappoint us.

Romans 5:4–5

God is often more patient with us than we are with ourselves. We assume that if we fall, we aren't born again. If we stumble, then we aren't truly converted. If we have the old desires, then we must not be a new creation.

If you are anxious about this, please remember, "God began doing a good work in you, and I am sure he will continue it until it is finished when Jesus Christ comes again" (Philippians 1:6).

A Gentle Thunder

August 13

Give God Your Worries

When I kept things to myself, I felt weak deep inside me.

Psalm 32:3

Ask yourself two questions:

Is there any unconfessed sin in my life?

Confession is telling God you did the thing he saw you do. He doesn't need to hear it as much as you need to say it. Whether it's too small to be mentioned or too big to be forgiven isn't yours to decide. Your task is to be honest.

Are there any unsurrendered worries in my heart?

"Give all your worries to him, because he cares about you" (1 Peter 5:7).

The German word for worry means "to strangle." The Greek word means "to divide the mind." Both are accurate. Worry is a noose on the neck and a distraction of the mind, neither of which is befitting for joy.

When God Whispers Your Name

August 14

What Are Your Strengths?

We all have different gifts, each of which came because of the grace God gave us.

Romans 12:6

There are some things we want to do but simply aren't equipped to accomplish. I, for example, have the desire to sing. Singing for others would give me wonderful satisfaction. The problem is, it wouldn't give the same satisfaction to my audience.

Paul gives good advice in Romans 12:3: "Have a sane estimate of your capabilities" (Phillips).

In other words, be aware of your strengths. When you teach, do people listen? When you lead, do people follow? When you administer, do things improve? Where are you most productive? Identify your strengths, and then . . . major in them. Failing to focus on our strengths may prevent us from accomplishing the unique tasks God has called us to do.

Just Like Jesus

August 15

The Temple of God's Spirit

You should know that your body is a temple for the Holy Spirit who is in you. You have received the Holy Spirit from God. So you do not belong to yourselves.

1 Corinthians 6:19

You will live forever in this body. It will be different, mind you. What is now crooked will be straightened. What is now faulty will be fixed. Your body will be different, but you won't have a different body. You will have this one. Does that change the view you have of it? I hope so.

God has a high regard for your body. You should as well. Respect it. I did not say worship it. But I did say respect it. It is, after all, the temple of God. Be careful how you feed it, use it, and maintain it. You wouldn't want anyone trashing your home; God doesn't want anyone trashing his. After all, it is his, isn't it?

When Christ Comes

August 16

God Sees Our Value

God does not see the same way people see. People look at the outside of a person, but the Lord looks at the heart.

1 Samuel 16:7

God sees us with the eyes of a Father. He sees our defects, errors, and blemishes. But he also sees our value.

What did Jesus know that enabled him to do what he did?

Here's part of the answer. He knew the value of people. He knew that each human being is a treasure. And because he did, people were not a source of stress but a source of joy.

In the Eye of the Storm

August 17

Spiritual Bankruptcy

God will show his mercy forever and ever to those who worship and serve him.

Luke 1:50

God does not save us because of what we've done. Only a puny god could be bought with tithes. Only an egotistical god would be impressed with our pain. Only a temperamental god could be satisfied by sacrifices. Only a heartless god would sell salvation to the highest bidders.

And only a great God does for his children what they can't do for themselves.

God's delight is received upon surrender, not awarded upon conquest. The first step to joy is a plea for help, an acknowledgment of moral destitution, an admission of inward paucity. Those who taste God's presence have declared spiritual bankruptcy and are aware of their spiritual crisis. . . . Their pockets are empty. Their options are gone. They have long since stopped demanding justice; they are pleading for mercy.

The Applause of Heaven

August 18

Look for His Likeness

He will keep his agreement of love for a thousand lifetimes for people who love him and obey his commands.

Deuteronomy 7:9

We are God's idea. We are his. His face. His eyes. His hands. His touch. We are him. Look deeply into the face of every human being on earth, and you will see his likeness. Though some appear to be distant relatives, they are not. God has no cousins, only children.

We are, incredibly, the body of Christ. And though we may not act like our Father, there is no greater truth than this: We are his. Unalterably. He loves us. Undyingly. Nothing can separate us from the love of Christ (Romans 8:38–39).

A Gentle Thunder

August 19

A Place of Permanence

The Lord will always lead you.

Isaiah 58:11

You've been there. You've escaped the sandy foundations of the valley and ascended his grand outcropping of granite. You've turned your back on the noise and sought his voice. You've stepped away from the masses and followed the Master as he led you up the winding path to the summit.

Gently your Guide invites you to sit on the rock above the tree line and look out with him at the ancient peaks that will never erode. "What is necessary is still what is sure," he confides. "Just remember:

"You'll go nowhere tomorrow that I haven't already been.

"Truth will still triumph.

"The victory is yours."

The sacred summit. A place of permanence in a world of transition.

The Applause of Heaven

August 20

Four Habits Worth Having

But grow in the grace and knowledge of our Lord and Savior Jesus Christ.

2 Peter 3:18 NIV

Growth is the goal of the Christian. Maturity is mandatory. If a child ceased to develop, the parent would be concerned, right?

When a Christian stops growing, help is needed. If you are the same Christian you were a few months ago, be careful. You might be wise to get a checkup. Not on your body, but on your heart. Not a physical, but a spiritual.

May I suggest one?

Why don't you check your habits? Make these four habits regular activities and see what happens.

First, the habit of prayer. Second, the habit of study. Third, the habit of giving. And last of all, the habit of fellowship.

When God Whispers Your Name

August 21

A Focus to Life

Work as if you were doing it for the Lord, not for people.

Colossians 3:23

When do we get our first clue that [Jesus] knows he is the Son of God? In the temple of Jerusalem. He is twelve years old. His parents are three days into the return trip to Nazareth before they notice he is missing. They find him in the temple studying with the leaders.

As a young boy, Jesus already senses the call of God. But what does he do next? Recruit apostles and preach sermons and perform miracles? No, he goes home to his folks and learns the family business.

That is exactly what you should do. Want to bring focus to your life? Do what Jesus did. Go home, love your family, and take care of business. *But Max, I want to be a missionary.* Your first mission field is under your roof. What makes you think they'll believe you overseas if they don't believe you across the hall?

Just Like Jesus

August 22

God Is on Our Team

When I was helpless, he saved me.

Psalm 116:6

As youngsters, we neighborhood kids would play street football. The minute we got home from school, we'd drop the books and hit the pavement. The kid across the street had a dad with a great arm and an addiction to football. As soon as he'd pull in the driveway from work, we'd start yelling for him to come and play ball. He couldn't resist. Out of fairness he'd always ask, "Which team is losing?" Then he would join that team, which often seemed to be mine.

His appearance in the huddle changed the whole ball game. He was confident, strong, and most of all, he had a plan. We'd circle around him, and he'd look at us and say, "Okay boys, here is what we are going to do." The other side was groaning before we left the huddle. You see, we not only had a new plan, we had a new leader.

He brought new life to our team. God does precisely the same. We didn't need a new play; we needed a new plan. We didn't need to trade positions; we needed a new player. That player is Jesus Christ, God's firstborn Son.

In the Grip of Grace

August 23

Perfected

Their sins and the evil things they do—I will not remember anymore.

Hebrews 10:17

With one sacrifice he made perfect forever those who are being made holy" (Hebrews 10:14).

Underline the word *perfect.* Note that the word is not better. Not improving. Not on the upswing. God doesn't improve; he perfects. He doesn't enhance; he completes.

Now I realize that there's a sense in which we're imperfect. We still err. We still stumble. We still do exactly what we don't want to do. And that part of us is, according to the verse, "being made holy."

But when it comes to our position before God, we're perfect. When he sees each of us, he sees one who has been made perfect through the One who is perfect—Jesus Christ.

In the Eye of the Storm

August 24

Set Apart

The Spirit produces the fruit of love, joy, peace, patience, kindness, goodness, faithfulness, gentleness, self-control.

Galatians 5:22–23

In the third century, St. Cyprian wrote to a friend named Donatus:

> *This seems a cheerful world, Donatus, when I view it from this fair garden. . . . But if I climbed some great mountain and looked out . . . you know very well what I would see; brigands on the high road, pirates on the seas, in the amphitheaters men murdered to please the applauding crowds. . . .*
>
> *Yet in the midst of it, I have found a quiet and holy people. . . . They are despised and persecuted, but they care not. They have overcome the world. These people, Donatus, are Christians.*

What a compliment! "A quiet and holy people."

Quiet. Not obnoxious. Not boastful. Not demanding. Just quiet.

Holy. Set apart. Pure. Decent. Honest. Wholesome.

The Inspirational Study Bible

August 25

Rescued by Heaven

I tell you the truth, whoever hears what I say and believes in the One who sent me has eternal life.

John 5:24

When you recognize God as Creator, you will admire him. When you recognize his wisdom, you will learn from him. When you discover his strength, you will rely on him. But only when he saves you will you worship him.

It's a "before and after" scenario. Before your rescue, you could easily keep God at a distance. Sure he was important, but so was your career. Your status. Your salary.

Then came the storm . . . the rage . . . the fight . . . the ripped moorings. Despair fell like a fog; your bearings were gone. In your heart, you knew there was no exit.

Turn to your career for help? Only if you want to hide from the storm . . . not escape it. Lean on your status for strength? A storm isn't impressed with your title.

Suddenly you are left with one option: God.

In the Eye of the Storm

August 26

Let the Redeemed Say So

You have begun to live the new life, in which you are being made new and are becoming like the One who made you.

Colossians 3:10

I wonder if Jesus doesn't muster up a slight smile as he sees his lost sheep come straggling into the fold—the beaten, broken, dirty sheep who stands at the door looking up at the Shepherd, asking, "Can I come in? I don't deserve it, but is there room in your kingdom for one more?" The Shepherd looks down at the sheep and says, "Come in, this is your home."

Salvation is the process that's done, that's secure, that no one can take away from you. Sanctification is the lifelong process of being changed from one degree of glory to the next, growing in Christ, putting away the old, taking on the new.

The psalmist David would tell us that those who have been redeemed will say so! If we're not saying so, perhaps it's because we've forgotten what it is like to be redeemed. "Let the redeemed of the Lord say so!" (Psalm 107:2 NASB).

Walking with the Savior

August 27

God Energizes Our Efforts

We proclaim him, admonishing and teaching everyone with all wisdom, so that we may present everyone perfect in Christ. To this end I labor, struggling with all his energy, which so powerfully works in me.

Colossians 1:28–29 NIV

Look at Paul's aim, *to present everyone perfect in Christ.* Paul dreamed of the day each person would be safe in Christ. What was his method? *Counseling and teaching.* Paul's tools? Verbs. Nouns. Sentences. Lessons. The same equipment you and I have.

Was it easier then than now? Don't think so. Paul called it work. "To this end I labor," he wrote. Labor means work. Work means homes visited, people taught, classes prepared.

How did he do it? What was his source of strength? He worked with all the energy he so powerfully works in me.

As Paul worked, so did God. And as you work, so does the Father.

When God Whispers Your Name

August 28

God Knows What's Best

Trust the Lord with all your heart, and don't depend on your own understanding.

Proverbs 3:5

The problem with this world is that it doesn't fit. Oh, it will do for now, but it isn't tailor-made. We were made to live with God, but on earth we live by faith. We were made to live forever, but on this earth we live but for a moment.

We must trust God. We must trust not only that he does what is best but that he knows what is ahead. Ponder the words of Isaiah 57:1–2: "The good men perish; the godly die before their time and no one seems to care or wonder why. No one seems to realize that God is taking them away from the evil days ahead. For the godly who die shall rest in peace" (TLB).

My, what a thought. "God is taking them away from the evil days ahead." Could death be God's grace? Could the funeral wreath be God's safety ring? As horrible as the grave may be, could it be God's protection from the future?

Trust in God, Jesus urges, and trust in me.

A Gentle Thunder

August 29

Changed to His Likeness

By his power to rule all things, he will change our simple bodies and make them like his own glorious body.

Philippians 3:21

What do we know about our resurrected bodies? They will be unlike any we have ever imagined.

Will we look so different that we aren't instantly recognized? Perhaps. (We may need name tags.) Will we be walking through walls? Chances are we'll be doing much more.

Will we still bear the scars from the pain of life? The marks of war. The disfigurements of disease. The wounds of violence. Will these remain on our bodies? That is a very good question. Jesus, at least for forty days, kept his. Will we keep ours? On this issue, we have only opinions, but my opinion is that we won't. Peter tells us that "by his wounds you have been healed" (1 Peter 2:24 NIV). In heaven's accounting, only one wound is worthy to be remembered. And that is the wound of Jesus. Our wounds will be no more.

When Christ Comes

August 30

The Courtroom of the World

"You will be my witnesses—in Jerusalem, in all of Judea, in Samaria, and in every part of the world."

Acts 1:8

We are witnesses. And like witnesses in a court, we are called to testify, to tell what we have seen and heard. And we are to speak truthfully. Our task is not to whitewash nor bloat the truth. Our task is to tell the truth. Period.

There is, however, one difference between the witness in court and the witness for Christ. The witness in court eventually steps down from the witness chair, but the witness for Christ never does. Since the claims of Christ are always on trial, court is perpetually in session, and we remain under oath.

Just Like Jesus

August 31

The Choice Is Ours

I will make you my promised bride forever. I will be good and fair; I will show you my love and mercy.

Hosea 2:19

For all its peculiarities and unevenness, the Bible has a simple story. God made man. Man rejected God. God won't give up until he wins him back.

God will whisper. He will shout. He will touch and tug. He will take away our burdens; he'll even take away our blessings. If there are a thousand steps between us and him, he will take all but one. But he will leave the final one for us. The choice is ours.

Please understand. His goal is not to make you happy. His goal is to make you his. His goal is not to get you what you want; it is to get you what you need.

A Gentle Thunder

SEPTEMBER

Let us hold firmly to the hope that we have confessed, because we can trust God to do what he promised.

—Hebrews 10:23

September 1

God Makes Us Right Again

Create in me a pure heart, God, and make my spirit right again.

Psalm 51:10

We are thirsty.

Not thirsty for fame, possessions, passion, or romance. We've drunk from those pools. They are saltwater in the desert. They don't quench—they kill.

"Blessed are those who hunger and thirst for righteousness" (Matthew 5:6 niv).

Righteousness. That's it. That's what we are thirsty for. We're thirsty for a clean conscience. We crave a clean slate. We yearn for a fresh start. We pray for a hand that will enter the dark cavern of our world and do for us the one thing we can't do for ourselves—make us right again.

The Applause of Heaven

September 2

Governed by Love

In Christ we are set free by the blood of his death, and so we have forgiveness of sins.

Ephesians 1:7

Jesus spoke of freedom, but he spoke of a different kind of freedom: the type of freedom that comes not through power but through submission. Not through control but through surrender. Not through possessions but through open hands.

God wants to emancipate his people; he wants to set them free. He wants his people to be not slaves but sons. He wants them governed not by law but by love.

We have been liberated from our own guilt and our own legalism. We have the freedom to pray and the freedom to love the God of our heart. And we have been forgiven by the only one who could condemn us. We are truly free!

Walking with the Savior

September 3
A Life Free of Clutter

"Your heart will be where your treasure is."

Matthew 6:21

The most powerful life is the most simple life. The most powerful life is the life that knows where it's going, that knows where the source of strength is, and the life that stays free of clutter and happenstance and hurriedness.

Being busy is not a sin. Jesus was busy. Paul was busy. Peter was busy. Nothing of significance is achieved without effort and hard work and weariness. Being busy, in and of itself, is not a sin. But being busy in an endless pursuit of things that leave us empty and hollow and broken inside—that cannot be pleasing to God.

One source of man's weariness is the pursuit of things that can never satisfy; but which one of us has not been caught up in that pursuit at some time in our life? Our passions, possessions, and pride—these are all dead things. When we try to get life out of dead things, the result is only weariness and dissatisfaction.

Walking with the Savior

September 4

God, Our Defender

He is my defender; I will not be defeated.

Psalm 62:6

Here is a big question. What is God doing when you are in a bind? When the lifeboat springs a leak? When the rip cord snaps? When the last penny is gone before the last bill is paid?

I know what we are doing. Nibbling on nails like corn on the cob. Pacing floors. Taking pills.

But what does God do?

He fights for us. He steps into the ring and points us to our corner and takes over. "Remain calm; the Lord will fight for you" (Exodus 14:14).

His job is to fight. Our job is to trust.

Just trust. Not direct. Or question. Our job is to pray and wait.

When God Whispers Your Name

September 5

Don't Panic

Let us hold firmly to the hope that we have confessed, because we can trust God to do what he promised.

Hebrews 10:23

Your disappointments too heavy? Read the story of the Emmaus-bound disciples. The Savior they thought was dead now walked beside them. He entered their house and sat at their table. And something happened in their hearts. "It felt like a fire burning in us when Jesus talked to us on the road and explained the Scriptures to us" (Luke 24:32).

Next time you're disappointed, don't panic. Don't give up. Just be patient and let God remind you he's still in control. It ain't over till it's over.

He Still Moves Stones

September 6

The Wages of Deceit

No one who is dishonest will live in my house; no liars will stay around me.

Psalm 101:7

More than once I've heard people refer to the story [of Ananias and Sapphira] with a nervous chuckle and say, "I'm glad God doesn't still strike people dead for lying." I'm not so sure he doesn't. It seems to me that the wages of deceit is still death. Not death of the body, perhaps, but the death of:

a marriage—Falsehoods are termites in the trunk of the family tree.
a conscience—The tragedy of the second lie is that it is always easier to tell than the first.
a career—Just ask the student who got booted out for cheating, or the employee who got fired for embezzlement if the lie wasn't fatal.

We could also list the deaths of intimacy, trust, peace, credibility, and self-respect. But perhaps the most tragic death that occurs from deceit is our [Christian] witness. The court won't listen to the testimony of a perjured witness. Neither will the world.

Just Like Jesus

September 7

God Loves the Truth

The Lord hates those who tell lies but is pleased with those who keep their promises.

Proverbs 12:22

Our Master has a strict honor code. From Genesis to Revelation, the theme is the same: God loves the truth and hates deceit. In 1 Corinthians 6:9–10 Paul lists the type of people who will not inherit the kingdom of God. The covey he portrays is a ragged assortment of those who sin sexually, worship idols, take part in adultery, sell their bodies, get drunk, rob people, and—there it is—*lie about others.*

Such rigor may surprise you. You mean my fibbing and flattering stir the same heavenly anger as adultery and aggravated assault? Apparently so.

Why the hard line? Why the tough stance?

For one reason: dishonesty is absolutely contrary to the character of God.

Just Like Jesus

September 8

Blessed Are the Focused

Each of you has received a gift to use to serve others.

1 Peter 4:10

There is only so much sand in the hourglass. Who gets it?

You know what I'm talking about, don't you?

"The PTA needs a new treasurer. With your background and experience and talent and wisdom and love for kids and degree in accounting, YOU are the perfect one for the job!"

It's tug-of-war, and you are the rope.

"Blessed are the meek," Jesus said. The word *meek* does not mean weak. It means *focused.* It is a word used to describe a domesticated stallion. Power under control.

Blessed are those who recognize their God-given responsibilities. Blessed are those who acknowledge that there is only one God and have quit applying for his position. Blessed are those who know what on earth they are on earth to do and set themselves about the business of doing it.

In the Eye of the Storm

September 9

Fear and Faith

About midnight Paul and Silas were praying and singing songs to God as the other prisoners listened.

Acts 16:25

Great acts of faith are seldom born out of calm calculation.

It wasn't logic that caused Moses to raise his staff on the bank of the Red Sea.

It wasn't medical research that convinced Naaman to dip seven times in the river.

It wasn't common sense that caused Paul to abandon the Law and embrace grace.

And it wasn't a confident committee that prayed in a small room in Jerusalem for Peter's release from prison. It was a fearful, desperate band of backed-into-a-corner believers. It was a church with no options. A congregation of have-nots pleading for help.

And never were they stronger.

At the beginning of every act of faith, there is often a seed of fear.

In the Eye of the Storm

September 10

Who Can Fathom Eternity?

God has planted eternity in the hearts of men.

Ecclesiastes 3:11 TLB

It doesn't take a wise person to know that people long for more than earth. When we see pain, we yearn. When we see hunger, we question why. Senseless deaths. Endless tears, needless loss.

We have our moments. The newborn on our breast, the bride on our arm, the sunshine on our back. But even those moments are simply slivers of light breaking through heaven's window. God flirts with us. He tantalizes us. He romances us. Those moments are appetizers for the dish that is to come.

"No one has ever imagined what God has prepared for those who love him" (1 Corinthians 2:9).

What a breathtaking verse! Do you see what it says? Heaven is beyond our imagination. At our most creative moment, at our deepest thought, at our highest level, we still cannot fathom eternity.

When God Whispers Your Name

September 11

From the Inside Out

"I will ask the Father, and he will give you another Helper to be with you forever—the Spirit of truth."

John 14:16–17

Do-it-yourself Christianity is not much encouragement to the done-in and worn-out.

Self-sanctification holds little hope for the addict.

At some point we need more than good advice; we need help. Somewhere on this journey home we realize that a fifty-fifty proposition is too little. We need more.

We need help. Help from the inside out. Not near us. Not above us. Not around us. But in us. In the part of us we don't even know. In the heart no one else has seen. In the hidden recesses of our being dwells not an angel, not a philosophy, not a genie, but God.

When God Whispers Your Name

September 12

The Ultimate Triumph

"Unless a grain of wheat falls into the earth and dies, it remains a single grain of wheat; but if it dies, it brings a good harvest."

John 12:24 Phillips

We do all we can to live and not die. God, however, says we must die in order to live. When you sow a seed, it must die in the ground before it can grow. What we see as the ultimate tragedy, he sees as the ultimate triumph.

And when a Christian dies, it's not a time to despair, but a time to trust. Just as the seed is buried and the material wrapping decomposes, so our fleshly body will be buried and will decompose. But just as the buried seed sprouts new life, so our body will blossom into a new body.

The seed buried in the earth will blossom in heaven. Your soul and body will reunite, and you will be like Jesus.

When Christ Comes

September 13

Sweeter After A Rest

In six days the Lord made everything. . . .
On the seventh day he rested.

Exodus 20:11

Time has skyrocketed in value. The value of any commodity depends on its scarcity. And time that once was abundant now is going to the highest bidder.

When I was ten years old, my mother enrolled me in piano lessons. Spending thirty minutes every afternoon tethered to a piano bench was a torture.

Some of the music, though, I learned to enjoy. I hammered the staccatos. I belabored the crescendos. . . . But there was one instruction in the music I could never obey to my teacher's satisfaction. The rest. The zigzagged command to do nothing. What sense does that make? Why sit at the piano and pause when you can pound?

"Because," my teacher patiently explained, "music is always sweeter after a rest."

It didn't make sense to me at age ten. But now, a few decades later, the words ring with wisdom—divine wisdom.

The Applause of Heaven

September 14

The Power of Your Hands

But those who do right will continue to do right, and those whose hands are not dirty with sin will grow stronger.

Job 17:9

What if someone were to film a documentary on your hands? What if a producer were to tell your story based on the life of your hands? What would we see? As with all of us, the film would begin with an infant's fist, then a close-up of a tiny hand wrapped around Mommy's finger. Then what? Holding on to a chair as you learned to walk? . . .

Were you to show the documentary to your friends, you'd be proud of certain moments: your hands extending with a gift, placing a ring on another's finger, doctoring a wound, preparing a meal. And then there are other scenes. Hands taking more often than giving, demanding instead of offering.

Oh, the power of our hands. Leave them unmanaged and they become weapons: clawing for power, strangling for survival, seducing for pleasure. But manage them and our hands become instruments of grace—not just tools in the hands of God, but God's very hands.

Just Like Jesus

September 15

To Tell the Truth

Speak the truth to one another.

Ephesians 4:25 tjb

Are you in a dilemma, wondering if you should tell the truth or not? The question to ask in such moments is: Will God bless my deceit? Will he, who hates lies, bless a strategy built on lies? Will the Lord, who loves the truth, bless the business of falsehoods? Will God honor the career of the manipulator? I don't think so either.

Examine your heart. Ask yourself some tough questions. Am I being completely honest with my spouse and children? Are my relationships marked by candor? What about my work or school environment? Am I honest in my dealings? Am I a trustworthy student? An honest taxpayer?

Do you tell the truth . . . always?

If not, start today. Don't wait until tomorrow. The ripple of today's lie is tomorrow's wave and next year's flood.

Just Like Jesus

September 16

WHAT A GOD!

LORD GOD All-Powerful, who is like you? LORD, you are powerful and completely trustworthy.

PSALM 89:8

PONDER THE ACHIEVEMENT OF GOD. HE DOESN'T condone our sin, nor does he compromise his standard.

He doesn't ignore our rebellion, nor does he relax his demands.
Rather than dismiss our sin, he assumes our sin and, incredibly, sentences himself.
God's holiness is honored. Our sin is punished . . . and we are redeemed.
God does what we cannot do so we can be what we dare not dream: perfect before God.

IN THE GRIP OF GRACE

September 17

God's Name in Your Heart

The name of the Lord is a strong tower;
the righteous run to it and are safe.

Proverbs 18:10 NKJV

When you are confused about the future, go to your *Jehovah-raah*, your caring shepherd. When you are anxious about provision, talk to *Jehovah-jireh*, the Lord who provides. Are your challenges too great? Seek the help of *Jehovah-shalom*, the Lord is peace. Is your body sick? Are your emotions weak? *Jehovah-rophe*, the Lord who heals you, will see you now. Do you feel like a soldier stranded behind enemy lines? Take refuge in *Jehovah-nissi,* the Lord my banner.

Meditating on the names of God reminds you of the character of God. Take these names and bury them in your heart.

God is

the shepherd who guides,
the Lord who provides,
the voice who brings peace in the storm,
the physician who heals the sick, and
the banner that guides the soldier.

The Great House of God

September 18

A Load Too Heavy

Do not be bitter or angry or mad. Never shout angrily or say things to hurt others.

Ephesians 4:31

Oh, the gradual grasp of hatred. Its damage begins like the crack in my windshield. Thanks to a speeding truck on a gravel road, my window was chipped. With time the nick became a crack, and the crack became a winding tributary. . . .

I couldn't drive my car without thinking of the jerk who drove too fast. Though I've never seen him, I could describe him. He is some deadbeat bum who cheats on his wife, drives with a six-pack on the seat, and keeps the television so loud the neighbors can't sleep.

Ever heard the expression "blind rage"?

Let me be very clear. Hatred will sour your outlook and break your back. The load of bitterness is simply too heavy. Your knees will buckle under the strain, and your heart will break beneath the weight. The mountain before you is steep enough without the heaviness of hatred on your back. The wisest choice—the only choice—is for you to drop the anger. You will never be called upon to give anyone more grace than God has already given you.

In the Grip of Grace

September 19

Imagine Seeing God

May the Lord bless you from Mount Zion,
he who made heaven and earth.

Psalm 134:3

The writer of Hebrew's gives us a *National Geographic* piece on heaven. Listen to how he describes the mountaintop of Zion. He says when we reach the mountain we will have come to "the city of the living God. . . . To thousands of angels gathered together with joy. . . . To the meeting of God's firstborn children whose names are written in heaven" (Hebrews 12:22–23).

What a mountain! Won't it be great to see the angels? To finally know what they look like and who they are?

Imagine the meeting of the firstborn. A gathering of all God's children. No jealousy. No competition. No division. We will be perfect . . . sinless.

And imagine seeing God. Finally, to gaze in the face of your Father. To feel the Father's gaze upon you. Neither will ever cease.

When God Whispers Your Name

September 20

Focus on God's Majesty

You have not seen Christ, but still you love him. You cannot see him now, but you believe in him.

1 Peter 1:8

Some years ago a sociologist accompanied a group of mountain climbers on an expedition. Among other things, he observed a distinct correlation between cloud cover and contentment. When there was no cloud cover and the peak was in view, the climbers were energetic and cooperative. When the gray clouds eclipsed the view of the mountaintop, though, the climbers were sullen and selfish.

The same thing happens to us. As long as our eyes are on God's majesty, there is a bounce in our step. But let our eyes focus on the dirt beneath us, and we will grumble about every rock and crevice we have to cross. For this reason Paul urged, "Don't shuffle along, eyes to the ground, absorbed with the things right in front of you. Look up, and be alert to the things going on around Christ—that's where the action is. See things from his perspective" (Colossians 3:1–2 msg).

The Great House of God

September 21
Guard the Gateway

The devil, your enemy, goes around like a roaring lion looking for someone to eat. Refuse to give in to him, by standing strong in your faith.

1 Peter 5:8–9

You've got to admit, some of our hearts are trashed out. Let any riffraff knock on the door, and we throw it open. Anger shows up, and we let him in. Revenge needs a place to stay, so we have him pull up a chair. Pity wants to have a party, so we show him the kitchen. Lust rings the bell, and we change the sheets on the bed. Don't we know how to say no?

Many don't. For most of us, thought management is, well, unthought of. We think much about time management, weight management, personnel management, even scalp management. But what about thought management? Shouldn't we be as concerned about managing our thoughts as we are managing anything else? Jesus was. Like a trained soldier at the gate of a city, he stood watch over his mind. He stubbornly guarded the gateway of his heart.

If he did, shouldn't we?

Just Like Jesus

September 22

Looking Up

Lord, show us the Father. That is all we need.

John 14:8

Biographies of bold disciples begin with chapters of honest terror. Fear of death. Fear of failure. Fear of loneliness. Fear of a wasted life. Fear of failing to know God.

Faith begins when you see God on the mountain and you are in the valley and you know that you're too weak to make the climb. You see what you need . . . you see what you have . . . and what you have isn't enough to accomplish anything.

Moses had a sea in front and an enemy behind. The Israelites could swim or they could fight. But neither option was enough.

Paul had mastered the Law. He had mastered the system. But one glimpse of God convinced him that sacrifice and symbols were not enough.

Faith that begins with fear will end up nearer the Father.

In the Eye of the Storm

September 23

Trust God with the Future

"Don't let your hearts be troubled. Trust in God, and trust in me."

John 14:1

Our [little] minds are ill-equipped to handle the thoughts of eternity. When it comes to a world with no boundaries of space and time, we don't have the hooks for those hats. Consequently, our Lord takes the posture of a parent, *Trust me.*

Don't be troubled by the return of Christ. Don't be anxious about things you cannot comprehend. For the Christian, the return of Christ is not a riddle to be solved or a code to be broken, but rather a day to be anticipated.

When Christ Comes

September 24
In the Arms of God

"Everyone who lives and believes in me will never die."

—John 11:26

We don't like to say good-bye to those whom we love. Whether it be at a school or a cemetery, separation is tough. It is right for us to weep, but there is no need for us to despair. They had pain here. They have no pain there. They struggled here. They have no struggles there. You and I might wonder why God took them home. But they don't. They understand. They are, at this very moment, at peace in the presence of God.

When it is cold on earth, we can take comfort in knowing that our loved ones are in the warm arms of God. And when Christ comes, we will hold them too.

When Christ Comes

September 25

The Best Is Yet to Be

"I will also give to each one who wins the victory a white stone with a new name written on it."

Revelation 2:17

Makes sense. Fathers are fond of giving their children special names. Princess. Tiger. Sweetheart. Bubba. Angel.

Isn't it incredible to think that God has saved a name just for you? One you don't even know? We've always assumed that the name we got is the name we will keep. Not so. The road ahead is so bright a fresh name is needed. Your eternity is so special no common name will do.

So God has one reserved just for you. There is more to your life than you ever thought. There is more to your story than what you have read.

And so I plead. Be there when God whispers your name.

When God Whispers Your Name

September 26
Radical Reconstruction

"Rejoice and be glad, because you have a great reward waiting for you in heaven."

Matthew 5:12

In the Sermon on the Mount, what Jesus promises is not a gimmick to give you goose bumps nor a mental attitude that has to be pumped up at pep rallies. No, Matthew 5 describes God's radical reconstruction of the heart.

Observe the sequence. First, we recognize we are in need (we're poor in spirit). Next, we repent of our self-sufficiency (we mourn). We quit calling the shots and surrender control to God (we're meek). So grateful are we for his presence that we yearn for more of him (we hunger and thirst). As we grow closer to him, we become more like him. We forgive others (we're merciful). We change our outlook (we're pure in heart). We love others (we're peacemakers). We endure injustice (we're persecuted).

It's no casual shift of attitude. It is a demolition of the old structure and a creation of the new. The more radical the change, the greater the joy. And it's worth every effort, for this is the joy of God.

The Applause of Heaven

September 27

God Knows What He's Doing

Surely I spoke of things I did not understand; I talked of things too wonderful for me to know.

Job 42:3

It's easy to thank God when he does what we want. But God doesn't always do what we want. Ask Job.

His empire collapsed, his children were killed, and what was a healthy body became a rage of boils. From whence came this torrent? From whence will come any help?

Job goes straight to God and pleaded his case. His head hurts. His body hurts. His heart hurts.

And God answered. Not with answers but with questions. An ocean of questions.

After several dozen questions, Job got the point. What is it?

The point is this: God owes no one anything. No reasons. No explanations. Nothing. If he gave them, we couldn't understand them.

God is God. He knows what he is doing. When you can't trace his hand, trust his heart.

The Inspirational Study Bible

September 28

The CEO of Heaven

Be careful what you think, because your thoughts run your life.

Proverbs 4:23

God wants you to "think and act like Christ Jesus" (Philippians 2:5). But how? The answer is surprisingly simple. We can be transformed if we make one decision: *I will submit my thoughts to the authority of Jesus.*

Jesus claims to be the CEO of heaven and earth. He has the ultimate say on everything, especially our thoughts. He has more authority, for example, than your parents. Your parents may say you are no good, but Jesus says you are valuable, and he has authority over parents.

Jesus also has authority over your ideas. Suppose you have an idea that you want to rob a grocery store. Jesus, however, has made it clear that stealing is wrong. If you have given him authority over your ideas, then the idea of stealing cannot remain in your thoughts.

To have a pure heart, we must submit all thoughts to the authority of Christ. If we are willing to do that, he will change us to be like him.

Just Like Jesus

September 29

Victory Over Death

Death, where is your victory? Death, where is your pain?

1 Corinthians 15:55

The fire that lit the boiler of the New Testament church was an unquenchable belief that if Jesus had been only a man, he would have stayed in the tomb. The earliest Christians couldn't stay silent about the fact that the one they saw hung on a cross walked again on the earth and appeared to five hundred people.

Let us ask our Father humbly, yet confidently in the name of Jesus, to remind us of the empty tomb. Let us see the victorious Jesus: the conqueror of the tomb, the one who defied death. And let us be reminded that we, too, will be granted that same victory!

Walking with the Savior

September 30

God, Our Father

Remember, O Lord, Your tender mercies and Your lovingkindnesses, for they are from of old.

Psalm 25:6 NKJV

Recently, my daughter Jenna and I spent several days in the old city of Jerusalem. One afternoon, as we were exiting the Jaffa gate, we found ourselves behind an orthodox Jewish family—a father and his three small girls. One of the daughters, perhaps four or five years of age, fell a few steps behind and couldn't see her father. "Abba!" she called to him. He spotted her and immediately extended his hand.

When the signal changed, he led her and her sisters through the intersection. In the middle of the street, he reached down and swung her up into his arms and continued their journey.

Isn't that what we all need? An abba who will hear when we call? Who will take our hand when we are weak? Who will guide us through the hectic intersections of life? Don't we all need an abba who will swing us up into his arms and carry us home? We all need a father.

The Great House of God

OCTOBER

We know the love that God has for us, and we trust that love.

—1 John 4:16

October 1

A Daily Blessing

I ask the Father in his great glory to give you the power to be strong inwardly through his Spirit.

Ephesians 3:16

Here is a scene repeated in Brazil thousands of times daily.

It's early morning. Time for young Marcos to leave for school. As he gathers his books and heads for the door, he pauses by his father's chair. He searches his father's face. *Benção, Pai?* Marcos asks. (Blessing, Father?)

The father raises his hand. *Deus te abençoe, meu filho*, he assures. (God bless you, my son.)

Father and child part for the day, a blessing requested, a blessing willingly given.

We should do the same. Like the child longing for the father's favor, each of us needs a daily reminder of our heavenly Father's love.

31 Days of Blessing

October 2

A Life of Service

We are many, but in Christ we are all one body. Each one is a part of that body.

Romans 12:5

God has enlisted us in his navy and placed us on his ship. The boat has one purpose—to carry us safely to the other shore.

This is no cruise ship; it's a battleship. We aren't called to a life of leisure; we are called to a life of service. Each of us has a different task. Some, concerned with those who are drowning, are snatching people from the water. Others are occupied with the enemy, so they man the cannons of prayer and worship. Still others devote themselves to the crew, feeding and training the crew members.

Though different, we are the same. Each can tell of a personal encounter with the captain, for each has received a personal call.

We each followed him across the gangplank of his grace onto the same boat. There is one captain and one destination. Though the battle is fierce, the boat is safe, for our captain is God. The ship will not sink. For that, there is no concern.

In the Grip of Grace

October 3

God's Highest Dream

It is not our love for God; it is God's love for us in sending his Son to be the way to take away our sins.

1 John 4:10

We have attempted to reach the moon but scarcely made it off the ground. We tried to swim the Atlantic, but couldn't get beyond the reef. We have attempted to scale the Everest of salvation, but have yet to leave the base camp, much less ascend the slope. The quest is simply too great. We don't need more supplies or muscle or technique; we need a helicopter.

Can't you hear it hovering?

"God has a way to *make people right with him*" (Romans 3:21, emphasis added). How vital that we embrace this truth. God's highest dream is not to make us rich, not to make us successful or popular or famous. God's dream is to make us right with him.

In the Grip of Grace

October 4

The Doorway to Your Heart

If people's thinking is controlled by the sinful self, there is death. But if their thinking is controlled by the Spirit, there is life and peace.

Romans 8:6

Your heart is a fertile greenhouse ready to produce good fruit. Your mind is the doorway to your heart—the strategic place where you determine which seeds are sown and which seeds are discarded. The Holy Spirit is ready to help you manage and filter the thoughts that try to enter. He can help you guard your heart.

He stands with you on the threshold. A thought approaches, a questionable thought. Do you throw open the door and let it enter? Of course not. You "fight to capture every thought until it acknowledges the authority of Christ" (2 Corinthians 10:5 Phillips). You don't leave the door unguarded. You stand equipped with handcuffs and leg irons, ready to capture any thought not fit to enter.

Just Like Jesus

October 5

We Need a Great Savior

[Peter] shouted, "Lord, save me!" Immediately Jesus reached out his hand and caught Peter.

Matthew 14:30–31

We come to Christ in an hour of deep need. We abandon the boat of good works. . . . We realize, like Peter, that spanning the gap between us and Jesus is a feat too great for our feet. So we beg for help. Hear his voice. And step out in fear, hoping that our little faith will be enough.

Faith is a desperate dive out of the sinking boat of human effort and a prayer that God will be there to pull us out of the water. Paul wrote about this kind of faith:

"For it is by grace you have been saved, through faith—and this not from yourselves, it is the gift of God—not by works, so that no one can boast" (Ephesians 2:8–9 NIV).

In the Eye of the Storm

Entering His Presence

For to me, to live is Christ and to die is gain.

PHILIPPIANS 1:21 NIV

JUST AS A PARENT NEEDS TO KNOW THAT HIS OR HER child is safe at school, we long to know that our loved ones are safe in death. We long for the reassurance that the soul goes immediately to be with God. But dare we believe it? Can we believe it? According to the Bible we can.

Scripture is surprisingly quiet about this phase of our lives. When speaking about the period between the death of the body and the resurrection of the body, the Bible doesn't shout; it just whispers. But at the confluence of these whispers, a firm voice is heard. This authoritative voice assures us that, at death, the Christian immediately enters into the presence of God and enjoys conscious fellowship with the Father and with those who have gone before.

When Christ Comes

October 7

Time Slips By

As many as walk according to this rule,
peace and mercy be upon them.

Galatians 6:16 NKJV

As we get older, our vision should improve. Not our vision of earth, but our vision of heaven. Those who have spent their life looking for heaven gain a skip in their step as the city comes into view. After Michelangelo died, someone found in his studio a piece of paper on which he had written a note to his apprentice. In the handwriting of his old age, the great artist wrote, "Draw, Antonio, draw, and do not waste time."

Well-founded urgency, Michelangelo. Time slips. Days pass. Years fade. Life ends. And what we came to do must be done while there is time.

He Still Moves Stones

October 8

Praise to God

Let us always offer to God our sacrifice of praise.

Hebrews 13:15

You are a great God.

Your character is holy.
Your truth is absolute.
Your strength is unending.
Your discipline is fair.
Your provisions are abundant for our needs.
Your light is adequate for our path.
Your grace is sufficient for our sins.
You are never early, never late.

You sent your Son in the fullness of time and will return at the consummation of time.

Your plan is perfect.
Bewildering. Puzzling. Troubling.
But perfect.

Safe in the Shepherd's Arms

October 9

A Home for Your Heart

Those who go to God Most High for safety
will be protected by the Almighty.

Psalm 91:1

Chances are you've given little thought to housing your soul. We create elaborate houses for our bodies, but our souls are relegated to a hillside shanty where the night winds chill us and the rain soaks us. Is it any wonder the world is so full of cold hearts?

Doesn't have to be this way. We don't have to live outside. It's not God's plan for your heart to roam as a Bedouin. God wants you to move in out of the cold and live . . . with him. Under his roof there is space available. At his table a plate is set. In his living room a wingback chair is reserved just for you. And he'd like you to take up residence in his house. Why would he want you to share his home?

Simple, he's your Father.

The Great House of God

October 10

Waiting Forwardly

The day of the Lord will come like a thief. The skies will disappear with a loud noise. . . . So what kind of people should you be?

2 Peter 3:10–11

Great question. What kind of people should we be? Peter tells us: "You should live holy lives and serve God, as you wait for and look forward to the coming of the day of God" (vv. 11–12).

Hope of the future is not a license for irresponsibility in the present. Let us wait forwardly, but let us wait.

But for most of us, waiting is not our problem. Or, maybe I should state, waiting is our problem. We are so good at waiting that we don't wait forwardly. We forget to look. We are too content. We seldom search the skies. We seldom, if ever, allow the Holy Spirit to interrupt our plans and lead us to worship so that we might see Jesus.

When Christ Comes

October 11

Finding Good in the Bad

Wish good for those who harm you; wish them well and do not curse them.

Romans 12:14

It would be hard to find someone worse than Judas. Some say he was a good man with a backfired strategy. I don't buy that. The Bible says, "Judas . . . was a thief" (John 12:6). The man was a crook. Somehow he was able to live in the presence of God and experience the miracles of Christ and remain unchanged.

In the end he decided he'd rather have money than a friend, so he sold Jesus for thirty pieces of silver. Judas was a scoundrel, a cheat, and a bum. How could anyone see him any other way?

I don't know, but Jesus did. Only inches from the face of his betrayer, Jesus looked at him and said, "Friend, do what you came to do" (Matthew 26:50). What Jesus saw in Judas as worthy of being called a friend, I can't imagine. But I do know that Jesus doesn't lie, and in that moment he saw something good in a very bad man.

He can help us do the same with those who hurt us.

Just Like Jesus

October 12

A Faithful Father

He is a faithful God who does no wrong, who is right and fair.

Deuteronomy 32:4

To recognize God as Lord is to acknowledge that he is sovereign and supreme in the universe. To accept him as Savior is to accept his gift of salvation offered on the cross. To regard him as Father is to go a step further. Ideally, a father is the one in your life who provides and protects. This is exactly what God has done.

He has provided for your needs (Matthew 6:25–34).

He has protected you from harm (Psalm 139:5).

He has adopted you (Ephesians 1:5). And he has given you his name (1 John 3:1).

God has proven himself as a faithful Father. Now it falls to us to be trusting children.

He Still Moves Stones

October 13

The Voice of Adventure

The Lord is my light and my salvation; whom shall I fear?

Psalm 27:1 NKJV

Jesus says the options are clear. On one side there is the voice of safety. You can build a fire in the hearth, stay inside, and stay warm and dry and safe. You can't get hurt if you never get out, right? You can't fall if you don't take a stand, right? You can't lose your balance if you never climb, right? So don't try it. Take the safe route.

Or you can hear the voice of adventure—God's adventure. Instead of building a fire in your hearth, build a fire in your heart. Follow God's impulses. Adopt the child. Move overseas. Teach the class. Change careers. Run for office. Make a difference. Sure it isn't safe, but what is?

He Still Moves Stones

October 14

Call It Grace

Being made right with God by his grace, we could have the hope of receiving the life that never ends.

Titus 3:7

You may be decent. You may pay taxes and kiss your kids and sleep with a clean conscience. But apart from Christ you aren't holy. So how can you go to heaven?

Only believe. Accept the work already done, the work of Jesus on the cross.

Accept the goodness of Jesus Christ. Abandon your own works and accept his. Abandon your own decency and accept his. Stand before God in his name, not yours.

It's that easy? There was nothing easy about it at all. The cross was heavy, the blood was real, and the price was extravagant.

It would have bankrupted you or me, so he paid it for us. Call it simple. Call it a gift. But don't call it easy.

Call it what it is. Call it grace.

A Gentle Thunder

October 15

God Is Your Home

"God is spirit, and those who worship him must worship in spirit and truth."

John 4:24

Don't think you are separated from God, he at the top end of a great ladder, you at the other. Dismiss any thought that God is on Venus while you are on earth. Since God is Spirit (John 4:24), he is next to you: God himself is our roof. God himself is our wall. And God himself is our foundation.

Moses knew this. "Lord," he prayed, "you have been our home since the beginning" (Psalm 90:1). What a powerful thought: God as your home. Your home is the place where you can kick off your shoes and eat pickles and crackers and not worry about what people think when they see you in your bathrobe.

Your home is familiar to you. No one has to tell you how to locate your bedroom. God can be equally familiar to you. With time you can learn where to go for nourishment, where to hide for protection, where to turn for guidance. Just as your earthly house is a place of refuge, so God's house is a place of peace. God's house has never been plundered; his walls have never been breached.

The Great House of God

October 16

A Treasure Map

In the beginning there was the Word. The Word was with God, and the Word was God.

John 1:1

The Bible has been banned, burned, scoffed, and ridiculed. Scholars have mocked it as foolish. Kings have branded it as illegal. A thousand times over, the grave has been dug and the dirge has begun, but somehow the Bible never stays in the grave. Not only has it survived, it has thrived. It is the single most popular book in all of history. It has been the best-selling book in the world for years!

There is no way on earth to explain it. Which perhaps is the only explanation. The answer? The Bible's durability is not found on earth; it is found in heaven. For the millions who have tested its claims and claimed its promises there is but one answer: the Bible is God's book and God's voice.

The purpose of the Bible is to proclaim God's plan and passion to save his children. That is the reason this book has endured through the centuries. . . . It is the treasure map that leads us to God's highest treasure: eternal life.

The Inspirational Study Bible

October 17

Salvation Celebration

"Rejoice that your names are written in heaven."

Luke 10:20 NIV

According to Jesus our decisions have a thermostatic impact on the unseen world. Our actions on the keyboard of earth trigger hammers on the piano strings of heaven. Our obedience pulls the ropes which ring the bells in heaven's belfries. Let a child call and the ear of the Father inclines. . . . And, most important, let a sinner repent, and every other activity ceases, and every heavenly being celebrates.

We don't always share such enthusiasm, do we? When you hear of a soul saved, do you drop everything and celebrate? Is your good day made better or your bad day salvaged? We may be pleased—but exuberant? When a soul is saved, the heart of Jesus becomes the night sky on the Fourth of July, radiant with explosions of cheer.

Can the same be said about us?

Just Like Jesus

October 18

The Gift of God's Smile

We do not make requests of you because we are righteous, but because of your great mercy.

Daniel 9:18 NIV

If only, when God smiles and says we are saved, we'd salute him, thank him, and live like those who have just received a gift from the commander in chief.

We seldom do that, though. We prefer to get salvation the old-fashioned way: we earn it. To accept grace is to admit failure, a step we are hesitant to take. We opt to impress God with how good we are rather than confessing how great he is. We dizzy ourselves with doctrine. Burden ourselves with rules. Think that God will smile on our efforts.

He doesn't.

God's smile is not for the healthy hiker who boasts that he made the journey alone. It is, instead, for the crippled leper who begs God for a back on which to ride.

In the Eye of the Storm

October 19

Confident in the Father

The Lord comforts his people and will have pity on those who suffer.

Isaiah 49:13

If you'll celebrate a marriage anniversary alone this year, [God] speaks to you.

If your child made it to heaven before making it to kindergarten, he speaks to you.

If your dreams were buried as they lowered the casket, God speaks to you.

He speaks to all of us who have stood or will stand in the soft dirt near an open grave. And to us he gives this confident word: "I want you to know what happens to a Christian when he dies so that when it happens, you will not be full of sorrow, as those are who have no hope. For since we believe that Jesus died and then came back to life again, we can also believe that when Jesus returns, God will bring back with him all the Christians who have died" (1 Thessalonians 4:13–14 TLB).

When Christ Comes

October 20

It's Called "Choice"

To choose life is to love the Lord your God,
obey him, and stay close to him.

Deuteronomy 30:20

He placed one scoop of clay upon another until a form lay lifeless on the ground.

All were silent as the Creator reached in himself and removed something yet unseen. It's called "choice." The seed of choice.

Within the man, God had placed a divine seed. A seed of his *self*. The God of might had created earth's mightiest. The Creator had created, not a creature, but another creator. And the One who had chosen to love had created one who could love in return.

Now it's our choice.

In the Eye of the Storm

October 21

Do Something

Faith that does nothing is dead!

James 2:26

Faith is not the belief that God will do what you want. Faith is the belief that God will do what is right. God is always near and always available. Just waiting for your touch. So let him know. Demonstrate your devotion:

Write a letter.
Ask forgiveness.
Be baptized.
Feed a hungry person.
Pray.
Teach.
Go.

Do something that demonstrates faith. For faith with no effort is no faith at all. God will respond. He has never rejected a genuine gesture of faith. Never.

He Still Moves Stones

October 22

A Crisp View of God

Lord, even when I have trouble all around me, you will keep me alive.

Psalm 138:7

There is a window in your heart through which you can see God. Once upon a time that window was clear. Your view of God was crisp. You could see God as vividly as you could see a gentle valley or hillside.

Then, suddenly, the window cracked. A pebble broke the window. A pebble of pain.

And suddenly God was not so easy to see. The view that had been so crisp had changed.

You were puzzled. God wouldn't allow something like this to happen, would he?

When you can't see him, trust him. Jesus is closer than you've ever dreamed.

In the Eye of the Storm

October 23

In a Word

He who overcomes, and keeps My works until the end, to him I will give power over the nations.

Revelation 2:26 NKJV

Think for a moment about this question: What if God weren't here on earth? You think people can be cruel now, imagine us without the presence of God. You think we are brutal to one another now, imagine the world without the Holy Spirit. You think there is loneliness and despair and guilt now, imagine life without the touch of Jesus. No forgiveness. No hope. No acts of kindness. No words of love. No more food given in his name. No more songs sung to his praise. No more deeds done in his honor. If God took away his angels, his grace, his promise of eternity, and his servants, what would the world be like?

In a word, hell.

Just Like Jesus

October 24

What Heaven Holds

"There is joy in the presence of the angels of God when one sinner changes his heart and life."

Luke 15:10

Why do Jesus and his angels rejoice over one repenting sinner? Can they see something we can't? Do they know something we don't? Absolutely. They know what heaven holds.

Heaven is populated by those who let God change them. Arguments will cease, for jealousy won't exist. Suspicions won't surface, for there will be no secrets. Every sin is gone. Every insecurity is forgotten. Every fear is past. Pure wheat. No weeds. Pure gold. No alloy. Pure love. No lust. Pure hope. No fear. No wonder the angels rejoice when one sinner repents; they know another work of art will soon grace the gallery of God. They know what heaven holds.

Just Like Jesus

October 25

No Secrets from God

If anyone belongs to Christ, there is a new creation. The old things have gone; everything is made new!

2 Corinthians 5:17

Have you been there? Have you felt the ground of conviction give way beneath your feet? The ledge crumbles, your eyes widen, and down you go. *Poof!*

Now what do you do? When we fall, we can dismiss it. We can deny it. We can distort it. Or we can deal with it.

We keep no secrets from God. Confession is not telling God what we did. He already knows. Confession is simply agreeing with God that our acts were wrong.

How can God heal what we deny? How can God grant us pardon when we won't admit our guilt? Ahh, there's that word: guilt. Isn't that what we avoid? Guilt. Isn't that what we detest? But is guilt so bad? What does guilt imply if not that we know right from wrong, that we aspire to be better than we are? That's what guilt is: a healthy regret for telling God one thing and doing another.

A Gentle Thunder

October 26

A Gentle Lamb

Where God's love is, there is no fear, because God's perfect love drives out fear.

1 John 4:18

A lot of us live with a hidden fear that God is angry at us. Somewhere, sometime, some Sunday school class or some television show convinced us that God has a whip behind his back, a paddle in his back pocket, and he's going to nail us when we've gone too far.

No concept could be more wrong! Our Savior's Father is very fond of us and only wants to share his love with us.

We have a Father who is filled with compassion, a feeling Father who hurts when his children hurt. We serve a God who says that even when we're under pressure and feel like nothing is going to go right, he is waiting for us, to embrace us whether we succeed or fail.

He doesn't come quarreling and wrangling and forcing his way into anyone's heart. He comes into our hearts like a gentle lamb, not a roaring lion.

Walking with the Savior

October 27

God's Faithfulness

My God will use his wonderful riches in Christ Jesus to give you everything you need.

Philippians 4:19

God's faithfulness has never depended on the faithfulness of his children. He is faithful even when we aren't. When we lack courage, he doesn't. He has made a history out of using people in spite of people.

Need an example? The feeding of the five thousand. It's the only miracle, aside from those of the final week, recorded in all four Gospels. Why did all four writers think it worth repeating? Perhaps they wanted to show how God doesn't give up even when his people do.

When the disciples didn't pray, Jesus prayed. When the disciples didn't see God, Jesus sought God. When the disciples were weak, Jesus was strong. When the disciples had no faith, Jesus had faith.

I simply think God is greater than our weakness. In fact, I think it is our weakness that reveals how great God is.

God is faithful even when his children are not.

A Gentle Thunder

October 28

A Heart Like His

From this time on we do not think of anyone as the world does.

2 Corinthians 5:16

Ask God to help you have his eternal view of the world. His view of humanity is starkly simple. From his perspective every person is either:

> Entering through the small gate or the wide gate (Matthew 7:13–14).
>
> Heaven called or hell bound (Mark 16:15–16).

Our ledger, however, is cluttered with unnecessary columns. Is he rich? Is she pretty? What work does he do? What color is her skin? Does she have a college degree? These matters are irrelevant to God.

To have a heart like his is to look into the faces of the saved and rejoice! They are just one grave away from being just like Jesus. To have a heart like his is to look into the faces of the lost and pray. For unless they turn, they are one grave away from torment.

Just Like Jesus

October 29

A Plate of Experiences

I have good plans for you, not plans to hurt you.

Jeremiah 29:11

Last night during family devotions, I called my daughters to the table and set a plate in front of each. In the center of the table, I placed a collection of food: some fruit, some raw vegetables, and some Oreo cookies. "Every day," I explained, "God prepares for us a plate of experiences. What kind of plate do you most enjoy?"

The answer was easy. Sara put three cookies on her plate. Some days are like that, aren't they? Some days are "three-cookie days." Many are not. Sometimes our plate has nothing but vegetables—twenty-four hours of celery, carrots, and squash. Apparently God knows we need some strength, and though the portion may be hard to swallow, isn't it for our own good? Most days, however, have a bit of it all.

The next time your plate has more broccoli than apple pie, remember who prepared the meal. And the next time your plate has a portion you find hard to swallow, talk to God about it. Jesus did.

The Great House of God

October 30

Love Is All You'll Find

We know the love that God has for us, and we trust that love.

1 John 4:16

Water must be wet. A fire must be hot. You can't take the wet out of water and still have water. You can't take the heat out of fire and still have fire.

In the same way, you can't take the love out of [God] and still have him exist. For he was, and is, Love.

Probe deep within him. Explore every corner. Search every angle. Love is all you find. Go to the beginning of every decision he has made and you'll find it. Go to the end of every story he has told and you'll see it.

Love.

No bitterness. No evil. No cruelty. Just love. Flawless love. Passionate love. Vast and pure love. He is love.

In the Eye of the Storm

October 31

Everyone Will See Him

"After I go and prepare a place for you, I will come back and take you to be with me so that you may be where I am."

John 14:3

Someday, according to Christ, he will set us free. He will come back.

In the blink of an eye, as fast as the lightning flashes from the east to the west, he will come back. And everyone will see him—you will, I will. Bodies will push back the dirt and break the surface of the sea. The earth will tremble, the sky will roar, and those who do not know him will shudder. But in that hour you will not fear, because you know him.

When Christ Comes

NOVEMBER

"Then you will know the truth, and the truth will make you free."

—JOHN 8:32

November 1

Take Jesus at His Word

In all these things we have full victory through God who showed his love for us.

Romans 8:37

When it comes to healing our spiritual condition, we don't have a chance. We might as well be told to pole-vault the moon. We don't have what it takes to be healed. Our only hope is that God will do for us what he did for the man at Bethesda—that he will step out of the temple and step into our ward of hurt and helplessness . . . which is exactly what he has done.

I wish we would take Jesus at his word.

When he says we're forgiven, let's unload the guilt.
When he says we're valuable, let's believe him.
When he says we're provided for, let's stop worrying.

God's efforts are strongest when our efforts are useless.

He Still Moves Stones

November 2

Sinner, Set Free

"Then you will know the truth, and the truth will make you free."

John 8:32

Think of it this way. Sin put you in prison. Sin locked you behind the bars of guilt and shame and deception and fear. Sin did nothing but shackle you to the wall of misery. Then Jesus came and paid your bail. He served your time; he satisfied the penalty and set you free. Christ died, and when you cast your lot with him, your old self died too.

The only way to be set free from the prison of sin is to serve its penalty. In this case the penalty is death. Someone has to die, either you or a heaven-sent substitute. You cannot leave prison unless there is a death. But that death has occurred at Calvary. And when Jesus died, you died to sin's claim on your life. You are free.

In the Grip of Grace

November 3

Are You Listening?

"Everyone who asks will receive. Everyone who searches will find."

Matthew 7:8

Once there was a man who dared God to speak: *Burn the bush like you did for Moses, God. And I will follow. Collapse the walls like you did for Joshua, God. And I will fight. Still the waves like you did on Galilee, God. And I will listen.*

And so the man sat by a bush, near a wall, close to the sea and waited for God to speak.

And God heard the man, so God answered. He sent fire, not for a bush, but for a church. He brought down a wall, not of brick, but of sin. He stilled a storm, not of the sea, but of a soul.

And God waited for the man to respond. And he waited . . . and waited.

But because the man was looking at bushes, not hearts; bricks and not lives, seas and not souls, he decided that God had done nothing.

Finally he looked to God and asked, *Have you lost your power?*

And God looked at him and said, *Have you lost your hearing?*

A Gentle Thunder

November 4

Run the Race

Let us run the race that is before us and never give up.

Hebrews 12:1

The word *race* is from the Greek *agon*, from which we get the word *agony.* The Christian's race is not a jog but rather a demanding and grueling, sometimes agonizing race. It takes a massive effort to finish strong.

Likely you've noticed that many don't? Surely you've observed there are many on the side of the trail? They used to be running. There was a time when they kept the pace. But then weariness set in. They didn't think the run would be this tough.

By contrast, Jesus' best work was his final work, and his strongest step was his last step. Our Master is the classic example of one who endured. He could have quit the race. But he didn't.

Just Like Jesus

November 5

Got It All Figured Out

I look at your heavens, which you made with your fingers. . . . But why are people even important to you?

Psalm 8:3–4

We understand how storms are created. We map solar systems and transplant hearts. We measure the depths of the oceans and send signals to distant planets. We have studied the systems and are learning how they work.

And, for some, the loss of mystery has led to the loss of majesty. The more we know, the less we believe. Strange, don't you think? Knowledge of the workings shouldn't negate wonder. Knowledge should stir wonder. Who has more reason to worship than the astronomer who has seen the stars?

Ironically, the more we know, the less we worship. We are more impressed with our discovery of the light switch than with the one who invented electricity. Rather than worship the Creator, we worship the creation (Romans 1:25).

No wonder there is no wonder. We've figured it all out.

In the Grip of Grace

November 6

The High Cost of Getting Even

Do not try to punish others when they wrong you, but wait for God to punish them with his anger.

Romans 12:19

Have you ever noticed in the western movies how the bounty hunter travels alone? It's not hard to see why. Who wants to hang out with a guy who settles scores for a living? Who wants to risk getting on his bad side? More than once I've heard a person spew his anger. He thought I was listening, when really I was thinking, *I hope I never get on his list.* Cantankerous sorts, these bounty hunters. Best leave them alone. Hang out with the angry and you might catch a stray bullet. Debt-settling is a lonely occupation. It's also an unhealthy occupation.

If you're out to settle the score, you'll never rest. How can you? For one thing, your enemy may never pay up. As much as you think you deserve an apology, your debtor may not agree. The racist may never repent. The chauvinist may never change. As justified as you are in your quest for vengeance, you may never get a penny's worth of justice. And if you do, will it be enough?

The Great House of God

November 7

God Loves You Dearly

We love because God first loved us.

1 John 4:19

Untethered by time, he sees us all. From the backwoods of Virginia to the business district of London; from the Vikings to the astronauts, from the cave-dwellers to the kings. From the hut-builders to the finger-pointers to the rock-stackers, he sees us. Vagabonds and ragamuffins all, he sees us before we are born.

And he loves what he sees. Flooded by emotion. Overcome by pride, the Starmaker turns to us, one by one, and says, "You are my child. I love you dearly. I'm aware that someday you'll turn from me and walk away. But I want you to know, I've already provided you a way back."

In the Grip of Grace

November 8

Finishing Strong

Think about Jesus' example. He held on while wicked people were doing evil things to him. So do not get tired and stop trying.

Hebrews 12:3

Heaven was not foreign to Jesus. He is the only person to live on earth *after* he had lived in heaven. As believers, you and I will live in heaven after time on earth, but Jesus did just the opposite. He knew heaven before he came to earth. He knew what awaited him upon his return. And knowing what awaited him in heaven enabled him to bear the shame on earth.

He "accepted the shame as if it were nothing because of the joy that God put before him" (Hebrews 12:2). In his final moments, Jesus focused on the joy God put before him. He focused on the prize of heaven. By focusing on the prize, he was able not only to finish the race but to finish it strong.

Just Like Jesus

November 9

A Compassionate God

He comforts us every time we have trouble, so when others have trouble, we can comfort them.

2 Corinthians 1:4

My child's feelings are hurt—I tell her she's special. My child is injured—I do whatever it takes to make her feel better. My child is afraid—I won't go to sleep until she is secure.

I'm not a hero. . . . I'm a parent. When a child hurts, a parent does what comes naturally. He helps.

Why don't I let my Father do for me what I am more than willing to do for my own children?

I'm learning. Being a father is teaching me that when I am criticized, injured, or afraid, there is a Father who is ready to comfort me. There is a Father who will hold me until I'm better, help me until I can live with the hurt, and who won't go to sleep when I'm afraid of waking up and seeing the dark.

Ever.

The Applause of Heaven

November 10

The Verdict

Jesus said [to her], "I also don't judge you guilty. You may go now, but don't sin anymore."

John 8:11

If you have ever wondered how God reacts when you fail, frame the words [of that verse] and hang them on the wall. Read them. Ponder them.

Or better still, take him with you to your canyon of shame. Invite Christ to journey with you . . . to stand beside you as you retell the events of the darkest nights of your soul.

And then listen. Listen carefully. He's speaking. "I don't judge you guilty."

And watch. Watch carefully. He's writing. He's leaving a message. Not in the sand, but on a cross.

Not with his hand, but with his blood.

His message has two words: "Not guilty."

He Still Moves Stones

November 11

He Wore Our Coat

They have washed their robes and made them white in the blood of the Lamb.

Revelation 7:14

God has only one requirement for entrance into heaven: that we be clothed in Christ.

Listen to how Jesus describes the inhabitants of heaven: "They will walk with me and will wear white clothes, because they are worthy" (Revelation 3:4).

Listen to the description of the elders: "Around the throne there were . . . twenty-four elders. . . . They were dressed in white and had golden crowns on their heads" (Revelation 4:4).

All are dressed in white. The saints. The elders. . . . How would you suppose Jesus is dressed? In white? . . . "He is dressed in a robe dipped in blood, and his name is the Word of God" (Revelation 19:13).

Why is Christ's robe not white? Why is his cloak not spotless? Why is his garment dipped in blood? Paul says simply, "He changed places with us" (Galatians 3:13).

He wore our coat of sin to the cross.

When Christ Comes

November 12

Honest with God

If you hide your sins, you will not succeed.

Proverbs 28:13

Our [high school] baseball coach had a firm rule against chewing tobacco. We had a couple of players who were known to sneak a chew, and he wanted to call it to our attention.

He got our attention, all right. Before long we'd all tried it. A sure test of manhood was to take a chew when the pouch was passed down the bench. I had barely made the team; I sure wasn't going to fail the test of manhood.

One day I'd just popped a plug in my mouth when one of the players warned, "Here comes the coach!" Not wanting to get caught, I did what came naturally, I swallowed. Gulp.

I added new meaning to the Scripture, "I felt weak deep inside me. I moaned all day long." I paid the price for hiding my disobedience.

My body was not made to ingest tobacco. Your soul was not made to ingest sin.

May I ask a frank question? Are you keeping any secrets from God? Take a pointer from a nauseated third baseman. You'll feel better if you get it out.

In the Grip of Grace

November 13

Saying "Thank You"

Thank the Lord because he is good. His love continues forever.

Psalm 106:1

Worship is when you're aware that what you've been given is far greater than what you can give. Worship is the awareness that were it not for his touch, you'd still be hobbling and hurting, bitter and broken. Worship is the half-glazed expression on the parched face of a desert pilgrim as he discovers that the oasis is not a mirage.

Worship is the "thank you" that refuses to be silenced.

We have tried to make a science out of worship. We can't do that. We can't do that any more than we can sell love or negotiate peace.

Worship is a voluntary act of gratitude offered by the saved to the Savior, by the healed to the Healer, and by the delivered to the Deliverer.

In the Eye of the Storm

November 14

A Place for the Weary

Do not lose the courage you had in the past, which has a great reward.

Hebrews 10:35

Is there anything more frail than a bruised reed? Look at the bruised reed at the water's edge. A once slender and tall stalk of sturdy river grass, it is now bowed and bent.

Are you a bruised reed? Was it so long ago that you stood so tall, so proud?

Then something happened. You were bruised . . .

by harsh words
by a friend's anger
by a spouse's betrayal.

The bruised reed. Society knows what to do with you. The world will break you off; the world will snuff you out.

But the artists of Scripture proclaim that God won't. Painted on canvas after canvas is the tender touch of a Creator who has a special place for the bruised and weary of the world. A God who is the friend of the wounded heart.

He Still Moves Stones

November 15

Fix Your Eyes on Jesus

May he enlighten the eyes of your mind so that you can see what hope his call holds for you.

Ephesians 1:18 TJB

What [does] it mean to be just like Jesus? The world has never known a heart so pure, a character so flawless. His spiritual hearing was so keen he never missed a heavenly whisper. His mercy so abundant he never missed a chance to forgive. No lie left his lips; no distraction marred his vision. He touched when others recoiled. He endured when others quit. Jesus is the ultimate model for every person. God urges you to fix your eyes upon Jesus. Heaven invites you to set the lens of your heart on the heart of the Savior and make him the object of your life.

Just Like Jesus

November 16

God Knows the Answers

If any of you needs wisdom, you should ask God for it.

James 1:5

Thomas came with doubts. Did Christ turn him away?

Moses had his reservations. Did God tell him to go home?

Job had his struggles. Did God avoid him?

Paul had his hard times. Did God abandon him?

No. God never turns away the sincere heart. Tough questions don't stump God. He invites our probing.

Mark it down: God never turns away the honest seeker. Go to God with your questions. You may not find all the answers, but in finding God, you know the One who does.

Walking with the Savior

November 17

Spiritual Life from the Spirit

Now we do not live following our sinful selves, but we live following the Spirit.

Romans 8:4

Perhaps your childhood memories bring more hurt than inspiration. The voices of your past cursed you, belittled you, ignored you. At the time, you thought such treatment was typical. Now you see it isn't.

And now you find yourself trying to explain your past. Do you rise above the past and make a difference? Or do you remain controlled by the past and make excuses?

Think about this. Spiritual life comes from the Spirit! Your parents may have given you genes, but God gives you grace. Your parents may be responsible for your body, but God has taken charge of your soul. You may get your looks from your mother, but you get eternity from your Father, your heavenly Father. And God is willing to give you what your family didn't.

When God Whispers Your Name

November 18

It's Your Choice

"If people want to follow me, they must give up the things they want. They must be willing even to give up their lives to follow me."

Mark 8:34

On one side stands the crowd. Jeering. Baiting. Demanding.

On the other stands a peasant. Swollen lips. Lumpy eye. Lofty promise.

One promises acceptance, the other a cross.

One offers flesh and flash, the other offers faith.

The crowd challenges, "Follow us and fit in."

Jesus promises, "Follow me and stand out."

They promise to please. God promises to save.

God looks at you and asks, "Which will be your choice?"

A Gentle Thunder

November 19

What Makes God, God?

If we are not faithful, he will still be faithful, because he cannot be false to himself.

2 Timothy 2:13 TEV

God's blessings are dispensed according to the riches of his grace, not according to the depth of our faith.

Why is that important to know? So you won't get cynical. Look around you. Aren't there more mouths than bread? Aren't there more wounds than physicians? Aren't there more who need the truth than those who tell it?

So what do we do? Throw up our hands and walk away? Tell the world we can't help them?

No, we don't give up. We look up. We trust. We believe. And our optimism is not hollow. Christ has proven worthy. He has shown that he never fails. That's what makes God, God.

A Gentle Thunder

November 20

Run to Jesus

If we live, we are living for the Lord, and if we die, we are dying for the Lord.

Romans 14:8

Do you wonder where you can go for encouragement and motivation? Go back to that moment when you first saw the love of Jesus Christ. Remember the day when you were separated from Christ? You knew only guilt and confusion and then—a light. Someone opened a door and light came into your darkness, and you said in your heart, "I am redeemed!"

Run to Jesus. Jesus wants you to go to him. He wants to become the most important person in your life, the greatest love you'll ever know. He wants you to love him so much that there's no room in your heart and in your life for sin. Invite him to take up residence in your heart.

Walking with the Savior

November 21

A Diligent Search

Anyone who comes to God must believe that he is real and that he rewards those who truly want to find him.

Hebrews 11:6

One translation renders Hebrews 11:6: "God . . . rewards those who earnestly seek him" (NIV). I like the King James translation: "He is a rewarder of them that *diligently* seek him" (emphasis added).

Diligently—what a great word. Be diligent in your search. Be hungry in your quest, relentless in your pilgrimage. Let this book be but one of dozens you read about Jesus. Step away from the puny pursuits of possessions and positions, and seek your king.

Don't be satisfied with angels. Don't be content with stars in the sky. Seek him out as the shepherds did. Long for him as Simeon did. Worship him as the wise men did. Do as John and Andrew did: ask for his address. Do as Matthew: invite Jesus into your house. Imitate Zacchaeus: Risk whatever it takes to see Christ.

Just Like Jesus

November 22

When God Says No

"Whoever comes to me will never be hungry, and whoever believes in me will never be thirsty."

John 6:35

There are times when the one thing you want is the one thing you never get.

You pray and wait.

No answer.

You pray and wait.

May I ask a very important question? What if God says no?

What if the request is delayed or even denied? When God says no to you, how will you respond? If God says, "I've given you my grace, and that is enough," will you be content?

Content. That's the word. A state of heart in which you would be at peace if God gave you nothing more than he already has.

In the Grip of Grace

November 23

A Passion for Excellence

In Christ Jesus, God made us to do good works, which God planned in advance for us to live our lives doing.

Ephesians 2:10

The push for power has come to shove. And most of us are either pushing or being pushed.

I might point out the difference between a passion for excellence and a passion for power. The desire for excellence is a gift of God, much needed in society. It is characterized by respect for quality and a yearning to use God's gifts in a way that pleases him.

But there is a canyon of difference between doing your best to glorify God and doing whatever it takes to glorify yourself. The quest for excellence is a mark of maturity. The quest for power is childish.

The Applause of Heaven

November 24

A True Family

"My true brother and sister and mother are those who do what God wants."

Mark 3:35

Does Jesus have anything to say about dealing with difficult relatives? Is there an example of Jesus bringing peace to a painful family? Yes, there is.

His own.

It may surprise you to know that Jesus had a family at all! You may not be aware that Jesus had brothers and sisters. He did. Quoting Jesus' hometown critics, Mark wrote, "[Jesus] is just the carpenter, the son of Mary and the brother of James, Joseph, Judas, and Simon. And his sisters are here with us" (Mark 6:3).

And it may surprise you to know that his family was less than perfect. They were. If your family doesn't appreciate you, take heart, neither did Jesus'. . . .

[Yet] he didn't try to control his family's behavior, nor did he let their behavior control his. He didn't demand that they agree with him. He didn't sulk when they insulted him. He didn't make it his mission to try to please them.

He Still Moves Stones

November 25

Heavenly Rewards

"When the master comes and finds the servant doing his work, the servant will be blessed."

Matthew 24:46

The stadium is packed today. Since Friday, [Mark] McGwire has hit not one or two home runs, but three. For thirty-seven years, no one could hit more than sixty-one homers in one season; now the St. Louis slugger has hit sixty-eight. And he isn't finished. The fans are on their feet before he comes to bat; they stay on their feet long after he crosses the plate.

Not everyone can be a Mark McGwire. For every million who aspire, only one achieves. The vast majority of us don't hit the big ball, don't feel the ticker tape, don't wear the gold medal, don't give the valedictory address.

And that's okay. We understand that in the economy of earth, there are a limited number of crowns.

The economy of heaven, however, is refreshingly different. Heavenly rewards are not limited to a chosen few, but "to all those who have waited with love for him to come again" (2 Timothy 4:8).

When Christ Comes

November 26

The Bridge of Confession

I said, "I will confess my sins to the Lord,"
and you forgave my guilt.

Psalm 32:5

Once there were a couple of farmers who couldn't get along with each other. A wide ravine separated their two farms, but as a sign of their mutual distaste for each other, each constructed a fence on his side of the chasm to keep the other out.

In time, however, the daughter of one met the son of the other, and the couple fell in love. Determined not to be kept apart by the folly of their fathers, they tore down the fence and used the wood to build a bridge across the ravine.

Confession does that. Confessed sin becomes the bridge over which we can walk back into the presence of God.

In the Grip of Grace

November 27

God Knows Us by Name

The Lord is my shepherd; I have everything I need.

Psalm 23:1

Sheep aren't smart. They tend to wander into running creeks for water, then their wool grows heavy, and they drown. They need a shepherd to lead them to "calm water" (Psalm 23:2). They have no natural defense—no claws, no horns, no fangs. They are helpless. Sheep need a shepherd with a "rod and . . . walking stick" to protect them (Psalm 23:4 ICB). They have no sense of direction. They need someone to lead them "on paths that are right" (Psalm 23:3).

So do we. We, too, tend to be swept away by waters we should have avoided. We have no defense against the evil lion who prowls about seeking whom he might devour. We, too, get lost.

We need a shepherd. We need a shepherd to care for us and to guide us. And we have one. One who knows us by name.

A Gentle Thunder

November 28

Nothing Less than Jesus

"I have obeyed my Father's commands, and I remain in his love. In the same way, if you obey my commands, you will remain in my love."

John 15:10

God rewards those who seek him. Not those who seek doctrine or religion or systems or creeds. Many settle for these lesser passions, but the reward goes to those who settle for nothing less than Jesus himself. And what is the reward? What awaits those who seek Jesus? Nothing short of the heart of Jesus. "And as the Spirit of the Lord works within us, we become more and more like him" (2 Corinthians 3:18 TLB).

Can you think of a greater gift than to be like Jesus? Christ felt no guilt; God wants to banish yours. Jesus had no bad habits; God wants to remove yours. Jesus had no fear of death; God wants you to be fearless. Jesus had kindness for the diseased and mercy for the rebellious and courage for the challenges. God wants you to have the same.

He wants you to be just like Jesus.

Just Like Jesus

November 29

Lay Down Your Cares

Praise the Lord, God our Savior, who helps us every day.

Psalm 68:19

Perhaps the heaviest burden we try to carry is the burden of mistakes and failures. What do you do with your failures?

Even if you've fallen, even if you've failed, even if everyone else has rejected you, Christ will not turn away from you. He came first and foremost to those who have no hope. He goes to those no one else would go to and says, "I'll give you eternity."

Only you can surrender your concerns to the Father. No one else can take those away and give them to God. Only you can cast all your anxieties on the one who cares for you. What better way to start the day than by laying your cares at his feet?

Walking with the Savior

November 30

Ponder the Love of God

I pray that you . . . will have the power to understand the greatness of Christ's love—how wide and how long and how high and how deep that love is.

Ephesians 3:18

There is no way our little minds can comprehend the love of God. But that didn't keep him from coming.

From the cradle in Bethlehem to the cross in Jerusalem, we've pondered the love of our Father. What can you say to that kind of emotion? Upon learning that God would rather die than live without you, how do you react? How can you begin to explain such passion?

In the Grip of Grace

DECEMBER

The ways of God are without fault.

—Psalm 18:30

December 1

The Winner's Circle

The Lord will reward everyone for whatever good he does, whether he is slave or free.

Ephesians 6:8 niv

For all we don't know about the next life, this much is certain. The day Christ comes will be a day of reward. Those who went unknown on earth will be known in heaven. Those who never heard the cheers of men will hear the cheers of angels. Those who missed the blessing of a father will hear the blessing of their heavenly Father. The small will be great. The forgotten will be remembered. The unnoticed will be crowned and the faithful will be honored.

The winner's circle isn't reserved for a handful of the elite, but for a heaven full of God's children who "will receive the crown of life that God has promised to those who love him" (James 1:12 niv).

When Christ Comes

December 2

God Is for You

He will rejoice over you.

Zephaniah 3:17

God is *for* you. Turn to the sidelines; that's God cheering your run. Look past the finish line; that's God applauding your steps. Listen for him in the bleachers, shouting your name. Too tired to continue? He'll carry you. Too discouraged to fight? He's picking you up. God is for you.

God is for you. Had he a calendar, your birthday would be circled. If he drove a car, your name would be on his bumper. If there's a tree in heaven, he's carved your name in the bark.

"Can a mother forget the baby at her breast and have no compassion on the child she has borne?" God asks in Isaiah 49:15 (NIV). What a bizarre question. Can you mothers imagine feeding your infant and then later asking, "What was that baby's name?" No. I've seen you care for your young. You stroke the hair, you touch the face, you sing the name over and over. Can a mother forget? No way. But "even if she could forget her children, I will not forget you," God pledges (Isaiah 49:15).

In the Grip of Grace

December 3

The Cure for Disappointment

The ways of God are without fault.

Psalm 18:30

When God doesn't do what we want, it's not easy. Never has been. Never will be. But faith is the conviction that God knows more than we do about this life and He will get us through it.

Remember, disappointment is cured by revamped expectations.

I like the story about the fellow who went to the pet store in search of a singing parakeet. Seems he was a bachelor and his house was too quiet. The store owner had just the bird for him, so the man bought it.

The next day the bachelor came home from work to a house full of music. He went to the cage to feed the bird and noticed for the first time that the parakeet had only one leg.

He felt cheated that he'd been sold a one-legged bird, so he called and complained.

"What do you want," the store owner responded, "a bird who can sing or a bird who can dance?"

Good question for times of disappointment.

He Still Moves Stones

December 4

The Soul Killer

The payment for sin is death.

Romans 6:23

Sin does to a life what shears do to a flower. A cut at the stem separates a flower from the source of life. Initially the flower is attractive, still colorful and strong. But watch that flower over a period of time, and the leaves will wilt and the petals will drop. No matter what you do, the flower will never live again. Surround it with water. Stick the stem in soil. Baptize it with fertilizer. Glue the flower back on the stem. Do what you wish. The flower is dead.

A dead soul has no life.

Cut off from God, the soul withers and dies. The consequence of sin is not a bad day or a bad mood but a dead soul. The sign of a dead soul is clear: poisoned lips and cursing mouths, feet that lead to violence and eyes that don't see God.

The finished work of sin is to kill the soul.

In the Grip of Grace

December 5

God's Thoughts

Lord, you have done such great things!
How deep are your thoughts!

Psalm 92:5

God's thoughts are not our thoughts, nor are they even like ours. We aren't even in the same neighborhood. We're thinking, *Preserve the body.* He's thinking, *Save the soul.* We dream of a pay raise. He dreams of raising the dead. We avoid pain and seek peace. God uses pain to bring peace. "I'm going to live before I die," we resolve. "Die, so you can live," he instructs. We love what rusts. He loves what endures. We rejoice at our successes. He rejoices at our confessions. We show our children the Nike star with the million-dollar smile and say, "Be like Mike." God points to the crucified carpenter with bloody lips and a torn side and says, "Be like Christ."

The Great House of God

December 6

A Heavenly Affirmation

I will be your father.

2 Corinthians 6:18

Each of us has a fantasy that our family will be like the Waltons, an expectation that our dearest friends will be our next of kin. Jesus didn't have that expectation. Look how he defined his family: "My true brother and sister and mother are those who do what God wants" (Mark 3:35).

When Jesus' brother didn't share his convictions, he didn't try to force them. He recognized that his spiritual family could provide what his physical family didn't.

We can't control the way our family responds to us. When it comes to the behavior of others toward us, our hands are tied. We have to move beyond the naive expectation that if we do good, people will treat us right. The fact is they may and they may not—we cannot control how people respond to us.

Let God give you what your family doesn't. If your earthly father doesn't affirm you, then let your heavenly Father take his place.

[And] don't lose heart. God still changes families.

He Still Moves Stones

December 7

No Worries in Heaven

[God] will wipe away every tear from their eyes, and there will be no more death, sadness, crying, or pain.

Revelation 21:4

What have you done today to avoid death? Likely a lot. You've popped pills, pumped pecks, passed on the pie, and pursued the polyunsaturates. Why? Why the effort? Because you are worried about staying alive. That won't be a worry in heaven.

In fact, you won't be worrying at all. Some of you moms worry about your kids getting hurt. You won't worry in heaven. In heaven we'll feel no pain. Some of you fellows worry about getting old. You won't in heaven. We'll all be ceaselessly strong.

We are not made of steel, we are made of dust. And this life is not crowned with life, it is crowned with death.

The next life, however, is different. Jesus urged the Christians in Smyrna to "be faithful, even if you have to die, and I will give you the crown of life" (Revelation 2:10).

When Christ Comes

December 8

Prayer Reminds Us

When a believing person prays, great things happen.

James 5:16

Prayer is the recognition that if God had not engaged himself in our problems, we would still be lost in the blackness. It is by his mercy that we have been lifted up. Prayer is that whole process that reminds us of who God is and who we are.

I believe there's great power in prayer. I believe God heals the wounded, and he can raise the dead. But I don't believe we tell God what to do and when to do it.

God knows that we, with our limited vision, don't even know that for which we should pray. When we entrust our requests to him, we trust him to honor our prayers with holy judgment.

Walking with the Savior

December 9

Grace upon Grace

I have learned to be satisfied with the things I have and with everything that happens.

Philippians 4:11

Test this question: What if God's only gift to you were his grace to save you. Would you be content? You beg him to save the life of your child. You plead with him to keep your business afloat. You implore him to remove the cancer from your body. What if his answer is "My grace is enough" (2 Corinthians 12:9). Would you be content?

You see, from heaven's perspective, grace is enough. If God did nothing more than save us from hell, could anyone complain? Having been given eternal life, dare we grumble at an aching body? Having been given heavenly riches, dare we bemoan earthly poverty?

If you have eyes to read these words, hands to hold this book, the means to own this volume, he has already given you grace upon grace.

In the Grip of Grace

December 10

Prepared Like a Bride

"The bride belongs only to the bridegroom."

John 3:29

John's descriptions of the future [in the book of Revelation] steal your breath. His depiction of the final battle is graphic. Good clashes with evil. The sacred encounters the sinful. The pages howl with the shrieks of dragons and smolder with the coals of fiery pits. But in the midst of the battlefield there is a rose. John describes it in chapter 21, verse 2:

> I saw the Holy City, the new Jerusalem, coming down out of heaven from God, prepared as a bride beautifully dressed for her husband.

In this final mountaintop encounter, God pulls back the curtain and allows the warrior to peek into the homeland. When given the task of writing down what he sees, John chooses the most beautiful comparison earth has to offer. The Holy City, John says, is like "a bride beautifully dressed for her husband" (NLT).

The Applause of Heaven

December 11

Just Pray

Anyone who is having troubles should pray.
Anyone who is happy should sing praises.

James 5:13

Do you want to know how to deepen your prayer life? Pray. Don't prepare to pray. Just pray. Don't read about prayer. Just pray. Don't attend a lecture on prayer or engage in discussion about prayer. Just pray.

Posture, tone, and place are personal matters. Select the form that works for you. But don't think about it too much. Don't be so concerned about wrapping the gift that you never give it. Better to pray awkwardly than not at all.

And if you feel you should only pray when inspired, that's okay. Just see to it that you are inspired every day.

When God Whispers Your Name

December 12

God Isn't Hard to Find

Surely goodness and mercy shall follow me all the days of my life. And I will dwell in the house of the Lord forever.

Psalm 23:6 NKJV

What a surprising way to describe God. A God who pursues us.

Dare we envision a mobile, active God who chases us, tracks us, following us with goodness and mercy all the days of our lives? He's not hard to find. He's there in Scripture, looking for Adam and Eve. They're hiding in the bushes, partly to cover their bodies, partly to cover their sin. Does God wait for them to come to him? No. The words ring in the garden. "Where are you?" God asks (Genesis 3:9), beginning his quest to redeem the heart of man. A quest to follow his children until his children follow him.

The Gift for All People

December 13

The Unspeakable Price

To all who did accept him and believe in him he gave the right to become children of God.

John 1:12

While we lived in Rio de Janeiro, we met several American families who came to Brazil to adopt children. They would spend days, sometimes weeks, immersed in a different language and a strange culture. They fought the red tape and paid the large fees, all with the hope of taking a child [home] to the United States.

Hasn't God done the same for us? He entered our culture, battled the resistance, and paid the unspeakable price which adoption required. Legally we are his. He owns us. We have every legal privilege accorded to [his] child. We are just waiting for him to return. We are, as Paul said, "waiting for God to finish making us his own children" (Romans 8:23).

When Christ Comes

December 14

EVERY CHILD HAS A NAME

"I am the good shepherd; I know my own sheep and my sheep know me as the Father knows me."

JOHN 10:14 NEB

THE SHEPHERD KNOWS HIS SHEEP. HE CALLS THEM by name.

When we see a crowd, we see exactly that: a crowd. We see people; not persons, but people. A herd of humans. A flock of faces. That's what we see.

But not so with the Shepherd. To him every face is different. Every face is a story. Every face is a child. Every child has a name.

The shepherd knows his sheep. He knows each one by name. The Shepherd knows you. He knows your name. And he will never forget it.

WHEN GOD WHISPERS YOUR NAME

December 15

A Broken Heart?

The Lord hates what evil people do, but he loves those who do what is right.

Proverbs 15:9

Perhaps the wound is old. A parent abused you. A teacher slighted you. A mate betrayed you. And you are angry.

Or perhaps the wound is fresh. The friend who owes you money just drove by in a new car. The boss who hired you with promises of promotions has forgotten how to pronounce your name. And you are hurt.

Part of you is broken, and the other part is bitter. Part of you wants to cry, and part of you wants to fight. There is a fire burning in your heart. It's the fire of anger.

And you are left with a decision. "Do I put the fire out or heat it up? Do I get over it or get even? Do I release it or resent it? Do I let my hurts heal, or do I let hurt turn into hate?"

Unfaithfulness is wrong. Revenge is bad. But the worst part of all is that, without forgiveness, bitterness is all that is left.

The Applause of Heaven

December 16

Words of Promise

God has given a son to us. . . . His name will be Wonderful Counselor, Powerful God . . . Prince of Peace.

Isaiah 9:6

Every Christmas I read this reminder that came in the mail several years ago:

> If our greatest need had been information, God would have sent an educator. If our greatest need had been technology, God would have sent us a scientist. If our greatest need had been money, God would have sent us an economist. But since our greatest need was forgiveness, God sent us a Savior.
>
> —Roy Lessin

Christmas cards. Punctuated promises. Phrases filled with the reason we do it all anyway . . .

He became like us, so we could become like him.
Angels still sing and the star still beckons.
He loves each one of us like there were only one of us to love.

When God Whispers Your Name

December 17

Because of Our Need

"For God did not send His Son into the world to condemn the world, but that the world through Him might be saved."

John 3:17 nkjv

Can you imagine prospective parents saying, "We'd like to adopt Johnny, but first we want to know a few things. Does he have a house to live in? Does he have money for tuition? Does he have a ride to school every morning and clothes to wear every day? Can he prepare his own meals and mend his own clothes?"

No agency would stand for such talk. Its representative would lift her hand and say, "Wait a minute. You don't understand. You don't adopt Johnny because of what he has; you adopt him because of what he needs. He needs a home."

The same is true with God. He doesn't adopt us because of what we have. He doesn't give us his name because of our wit or wallet or good attitude. Adoption is something we receive, not something we earn.

The Great House of God

December 18

Room for God?

"Here I am! I stand at the door and knock."

Revelation 3:20

Some of the saddest words on earth are "We don't have room for you."

Jesus knew the sound of those words. He was still in Mary's womb when the innkeeper said, "We don't have room for you."

And when he was hung on the cross, wasn't the message one of utter rejection? "We don't have room for you in this world."

Even today Jesus is given the same treatment. He goes from heart to heart, asking if he might enter.

Every so often, he is welcomed. Someone throws open the door of his or her heart and invites him to stay. And to that person Jesus gives this great promise: "In my Father's house are many rooms"(John 14:2 NKJV).

What a delightful promise he makes us! We make room for him in our hearts, and he makes room for us in his house.

When Christ Comes

December 19

Down on Your Knees

God is against the proud, but he gives grace to the humble.

James 4:6

A small cathedral outside Bethlehem marks the supposed birthplace of Jesus. Behind a high altar in the church is a cave, a little cavern lit by silver lamps.

You can enter the main edifice and admire the ancient church. You can also enter the quiet cave where a star embedded in the floor recognizes the birth of the King. There is one stipulation, however. You have to stoop. The door is so low you can't go in standing up.

The same is true of the Christ. You can see the world standing tall, but to witness the Savior, you have to get [down] on your knees.

The Applause of Heaven

December 20

The Gift Is God-Given

Every good action and every perfect gift is from God. These good gifts come down from the Creator of the sun, moon, and stars, who does not change like their shifting shadows.

James 1:17

The conclusion is unavoidable: self-salvation simply does not work. Man has no way to save himself.

But Paul announces that God has a way. Where man fails, God excels. Salvation comes from heaven downward, not earth upward. "Every good action and every perfect gift is from God" (James 1:17).

Please note: Salvation is God-given, God-driven, God-empowered, and God-originated. The gift is not from man to God. It is from God to man.

In the Grip of Grace

December 21

AN *EXTRA*-ORDINARY NIGHT

Today your Savior was born in the town of David. He is Christ, the Lord.

LUKE 2:11

AN ORDINARY NIGHT WITH ORDINARY SHEEP AND ordinary shepherds. And were it not for a God who loves to hook an "extra" on the front of the ordinary, the night would have gone unnoticed. The sheep would have been forgotten, and the shepherds would have slept the night away.

But God dances amidst the common. And that night he did a waltz.

The black sky exploded with brightness. Trees that had been shadows jumped into clarity. Sheep that had been silent became a chorus of curiosity. One minute the shepherd was dead asleep, the next he was rubbing his eyes and staring into the face of an alien.

The night was ordinary no more.

The angel came in the night because that is when lights are best seen and that is when they are most needed. God comes into the common for the same reason. His most powerful tools are the simplest.

THE APPLAUSE OF HEAVEN

December 22

The Gift of Grace

Those who find me find life, and the
Lord will be pleased with them.

Proverbs 8:35

Grace is created by God and given to man. On the basis of this point alone, Christianity is set apart from any other religion in the world. . . . Every other approach to God is a bartering system: If I do this, God will do that." I'm either saved by works (what I do), emotions (what I experience), or knowledge (what I know).

By contrast, Christianity has no whiff of negotiation at all. Man is not the negotiator; indeed, man has no grounds from which to negotiate.

In the Grip of Grace

December 23

God's Great Gifts

Thanks be to God for his gift that is too wonderful for words.

2 Corinthians 9:15

Why did he do it? A shack would have sufficed, but he gave us a mansion. Did he have to give the birds a song and the mountains a peak? Was he required to put stripes on the zebra and the hump on the camel? Why wrap creation in such splendor? Why go to such trouble to give such gifts?

Why do you? You do the same. I've seen you searching for a gift. I've seen you stalking the malls and walking the aisles. I'm not talking about the obligatory gifts. I'm talking about that extra-special person and that extra-special gift. Why do you do it? You do it so the heart will stop. You do it so the jaw will drop. You do it to hear those words of disbelief "You did this for me?"

That's why you do it. And that is why God did it. Next time a sunrise steals your breath or a meadow of flowers leaves you speechless, remain that way. Say nothing and listen as heaven whispers, "Do you like it? I did it just for you."

The Great House of God

December 24

The Promise Remains

Joseph was the husband of Mary, and Mary was the mother of Jesus. Jesus is called the Christ.

Matthew 1:16

Seems like the only common bond between [Jesus' ancestors] was a promise. A promise from heaven that God would use them to send his Son.

Why did God use these people? Didn't have to. Could have just laid the Savior on a doorstep. Would have been simpler that way. And why does God tell us their stories?

Simple. He wants us to know that when the world goes wild, he stays calm.

Want proof? Read the last name on the list [of Jesus' lineage]. In spite of all the crooked halos and tasteless gambols of his people, the last name on the list is the first one promised—Jesus.

No more names are listed. No more are needed. As if God is announcing to a doubting world, "See, I did it. Just like I said I would."

When God Whispers Your Name

December 25

God Became a Man

He gave up his place with God and made himself nothing.
He was born as a man and became like a servant.

Philippians 2:7

It all happened in a most remarkable moment . . . a moment like no other.

God became a man. Divinity arrived. Heaven opened herself and placed her most precious one in a human womb.

The omnipotent, in one instant, became flesh and blood. The one who was larger than the universe became a microscopic embryo. And he who sustains the world with a word chose to be dependent upon the nourishment of a young girl.

God had come near.

God Came Near

December 26

The Strength of God's Love

God shows his great love for us in this way: Christ died for us while we were still sinners.

Romans 5:8

Can anything make me stop loving you?" God asks. "Watch me speak your language, sleep on your earth, and feel your hurts. Behold the maker of sight and sound as he sneezes, coughs, and blows his nose. You wonder if I understand how you feel? Look into the dancing eyes of the kid in Nazareth; that's God walking to school. Ponder the toddler at Mary's table; that's God spilling his milk.

"You wonder how long my love will last? Find your answer on a splintered cross, on a craggy hill. That's me you see up there, your maker, your God, nail-stabbed and bleeding. Covered in spit and sin-soaked.

"That's your sin I'm feeling. That's your death I'm dying. That's your resurrection I'm living. That's how much I love you."

In the Grip of Grace

December 27

Admission into Joy

You . . . clothed me in happiness.

Psalm 30:11

The first step to joy is a plea for help, an acknowledgment of moral destitution, an admission of inward paucity. Those who taste God's presence have declared spiritual bankruptcy and are aware of their spiritual crisis. Their cupboards are bare. Their pockets are empty. Their options are gone. They have long since stopped demanding justice; they are pleading for mercy. . . .

They ask God to do for them what they can't do without him. They have seen how holy God is and how sinful they are and have agreed with Jesus' statement, "Salvation is impossible."

Oh, the irony of God's delight—born in the parched soil of destitution rather than the fertile ground of achievement.

It's a different path, a path we're not accustomed to taking. We don't often declare our impotence. Admission of failure is not usually admission into joy. Complete confession is not commonly followed by total pardon. But then again, God has never been governed by what is common.

The Applause of Heaven

December 28

Immersed in Grace

He called you to share in his glory in Christ,
a glory that will continue forever.

1 Peter 5:10

To believe we are totally and eternally debt free is seldom easy. Even if we've stood before the throne and heard it from the King himself, we still doubt. As a result, many are forgiven only a little, not because the grace of the King is limited, but because the faith of the sinner is small. God is willing to forgive all. He's willing to wipe the slate completely clean. He guides us to a pool of mercy and invites us to bathe. Some plunge in, but others just touch the surface. They leave feeling unforgiven.

Where the grace of God is missed, bitterness is born. But where the grace of God is embraced, forgiveness flourishes.

The more we immerse ourselves in grace, the more likely we are to give grace.

In the Grip of Grace

December 29

God Changes Families

"They all continued praying together with some women, including Mary the mother of Jesus, and Jesus' brothers."

Acts 1:14

God has proven himself as a faithful Father. Now it falls to us to be trusting children. Let God give you what your family doesn't. Let him fill the void others have left. Rely upon him for your affirmation and encouragement. Look at Paul's words: "You are God's child, and *God will give you the blessing he promised,* because you are his child" (Galatians 4:7, emphasis added).

Having your family's approval is desirable but not necessary for happiness and not always possible. Jesus did not let the difficult dynamic of his family overshadow his call from God. And because he didn't, [his family] chapter has a happy ending.

He gave them space, time, and grace. And because he did, they changed. One brother became an apostle (Galatians 1:19), and others became missionaries (1 Corinthians 9:5).

He Still Moves Stones

December 30

Our Goal

"All I have is yours, and all you have is mine.
And my glory is shown through them."

John 17:10

God is in the business of changing the face of the world.

Let me be very clear. This change is his job, not ours. Our goal is not to make our faces radiant. Not even Jesus did that. Matthew says, "Jesus' appearance was changed (17:2)" not "Jesus changed his appearance." Moses didn't even know his face was shining (Exodus 34:29). Our goal is not to conjure up some fake, frozen expression. Our goal is simply to stand before God with a prepared and willing heart and then let God do his work.

And he does. He wipes away the tears. He mops away the perspiration. He softens our furrowed brows. He touches our cheeks. He changes our faccs as we worship.

Just Like Jesus

December 31

Wistful Words

"I leave you peace; my peace I give you. I do not give it to you as the world does. So don't let your hearts be troubled or afraid."

John 14:27

If only you knew that I came to help and not condemn. If only you knew that tomorrow will be better than today. If only you knew the gift I have brought: eternal life. If only you knew I want you safely home.

If only you knew.

What wistful words to come from the lips of God. How kind that he would let us hear them. How crucial that we pause to hear them. If only we knew to trust. Trust that God is in our corner. Trust that God wants what is best.

If only we could learn to trust him.

A Gentle Thunder

Acknowledgments

Grateful acknowledgment is made to the following publishers for permission to reprint this copyrighted material. All copyrights are held by the author, Max Lucado.

The Applause of Heaven (Nashville: Word, 1990).
In the Eye of the Storm (Nashville: Word, 1991).
He Still Moves Stones (Nashville: Word, 1993).
Walking with the Savior (Wheaton: Tyndale House, 1993).
How to Study the Bible (Nashville: Word, 1994).
When God Whispers Your Name (Nashville: Word, 1994).
31 Days of Blessing (MaxLucado.com, 1995).
A Gentle Thunder (Nashville: Word, 1995).
The Inspirational Study Bible (Nashville: W Publishing Group, 1995).
In the Grip of Grace (Nashville: Word, 1996).
The Great House of God (Nashville: Word, 1997).
Just Like Jesus (Nashville: Word, 1998).
The Gift for All People (Sisters, OR: Multnomah Publishers, Inc., 1999).
When Christ Comes (Nashville: Word, 1999).
Safe in the Shepherd's Arms (Nashville: Thomas

Nelson, 2002).
And the Angels Were Silent (Nashville: W Publishing Group, 2003).
God Came Near (Nashville: W Publishing Group, 2003).
No Wonder They Call Him the Savior (Nashville: W Publishing Group, 2003).
Six Hours One Friday (Nashville: W Publishing Group, 2003).